ACKNOWLEDGEMENTS

There are many people to whom I am indebted in bringing this book to press.

I wish to affirm my appreciation for the Linenhall Library, Belfast and the unfailing helpfulness of its librarians. Without complaint they handled my almost daily requests for heavy bound volumes of newspaper archives to be carried from the store to my work place on the library's fourth floor. They were also kind to take an interest in my research. To my proof-readers I am also very indebted for their time and energy, perceptive critiques and advice.

Others have written excellent books on the political and economic problems of Northern Ireland in the 1950s. In writing this book I have not aimed at an academic analysis of the decade but instead tried to pick up on the weft and web of people's ordinary daily experiences. Someone once said that newspapers are the first draft of history so, it was to Belfast's morning dailies that I turned.

I literally scoured them to get a feel for what it was like to live through the '50s. My principal source has been the "Belfast Newsletter." It is, like its morning counterpart the "Irish News", jam- packed with stories on both world and local events and generally what life was like in the new era of H-bombs, Cold War and Sci-fi. Local stories of housing problems and scandals, unemployment troubles, entertainments, holidays, shops, tragedies and disasters, schooling and the nit-picking of politics are all there. So are the photos and advertisements which also capture the era.

My deep thanks go to the "Belfast Newsletter" for allowing me to use this material in my book.

This book is dedicated to my family and friends and in particular to Jean and Rosamond.

CONTENTS

INTRODUCTION

A S SOMEONE ONCE POINTED out the past can be like a foreign country where they do things differently. So, best to begin with a bit of potted history

The 1950s in Belfast squeezed as it was between the Blitz, the devastation of wartime and the even greater trauma of the "The Troubles" is a decade that has tended to get overlooked. Judgements about this period in the history of Northern Ireland argue that it was Northern Ireland's most successful and peaceful decade. Perhaps these judgements are made in comparison to the challenging times which followed and which led to the collapse of Stormont rule. Certainly all was not plain sailing at the start of the '50s.

Britain had emerged from World War Two far from unscathed and Belfast like its counterparts, the industrial cities on the mainland, shared in the post-war period of struggle against poverty, homelessness, industrial decline and unemployment. There were shortages of everything and wartime rationing continued for quite some time. In social and economic terms what adjectives spring to mind when remembering 1950s Belfast- grey, grim, austere? Post- war, it was a city of bombsites and in many areas slums.

The '50s hold in embryo those issues which were to have such

A cheer for the Premier

a profound effect on Belfast and Northern Ireland in the decades to follow. Chief of these are the political control of the province plus the decisions made in an effort to sort out Belfast's chronic housing problems, the out workings of the 1948 Acts setting up the Welfare State and Health Service and the new Education Orders

Basil Brooke [created Lord Brookeborough in 1952] had become Prime Minister of Northern Ireland in 1943. It was a position he was to hold until 1963. In his first speech as Prime Minister he outlined what his vision was for the future role of the Stormont government,

"to maintain the existing constitutional position of Northern Ireland, to bring the utmost vigour to the task of assisting the war effort..... and to make further preparation for dealing with the problems of the post – war period."

Brooke, from the beginning, was no reforming new broom. He was dyed in the wool unionist aristocracy and his attitude towards relations with the nationalist minority within Northern Ireland and the relationship between Northern Ireland and the rest of the island set much of the tone for the 1950s. Indeed, his modus operandi was not unlike that of a nineteenth century Austrian emperor who declared he wished to rule but change nothing.

Stormont buildings still dominate the landscape of East Belfast. A large imposing white stone structure in neo-Georgian style it symbolised in the 50s and 60s the solidity of unionist power in Northern Ireland.

The old Stormont legislature consisted of two houses, the upper house - the Senate -and the lower house -the Commons. The job of the Stormont Parliament was to take charge of regional matters.

The Crown was represented by the Governor of Northern Ireland. There were twenty-six Senators; twenty four elected by the House of Commons and two ex-officio members, the Lord Mayors of Belfast and Londonderry. Senators were elected for a term of eight years with half standing for re-election every fourth year.

There were 52 MPs in the old Stormont parliament. Forty-eight elected for separate constituencies and amazingly four for the university constituency. Entitlement to a vote was tied to rateable property. A voter with business premises could acquire up to six votes!

An additional qualification for a vote also had to be met. A voter had to be a British citizen born in Northern Ireland or to have been resident there for up to seven years. The unionists were not having any would be voters floating in from the Irish Republic. As well as a parliament at Stormont which was empowered to legislate on local matters the Ulster voter elected representatives to the central government at Westminster. Throughout the 1950s unionists held 8 out of the 12 Westminster seats.

The 1945 General Election in Britain had resulted in a landslide victory for Labour, a party the unionists suspected was less sensitive to their cause than the British Conservatives. The sense of insecurity created by the Labour victory produced a wariness from the unionists whose Westminster MPs had traditionally taken the Conservative Whip.

An example of this was the tension which arose between Labour -led Westminster and Unionist Stormont over the move by the Westminster government to change the franchise entitlement. Westminster in 1949 extended the vote to all of the adult population over the age of 21 years.

No parallel action was carried out at Stormont. The local government vote in Northern Ireland remained firmly tied to property. This failure to act in tandem with Westminster went on to produce the situation which eventually gave the Northern Ireland Civil Rights movement of the 1960s its resonant slogan, "One Man – One Vote."

Another problem arose over the introduction of post-war social and economic reform. The direction of social policy in post-war Britain had been shaped by the Beveridge Report of 1942. It had set out proposals for the development of those social and economic policies which would lead to the creation of the Welfare State. The people of Northern Ireland, relying on the principle of parity with the rest of Great Britain, looked forward to their equal share of the promised benefits. However, they had to wait longer than their counterparts on the mainland. The Northern Ireland government said it could not possibly meet the cost of providing for the new proposed services thus a gap of a few years occurred before the reforms were brought in paid for by an increase in funding by Westminster. This cry of disadvantage and the need to see Ulster as a special case was a theme of the Stormont administration's relationship with Her Majesty's Treasury.

The economy of the Irish Republic could not hope to rival these new wide ranging measures and a National Health Service as comprehensive as that of Northern Ireland's. From a unionist perspective clear blue water had developed between the standard of living in Northern Ireland and that in the Republic and unionists now felt they had a forceful argument for the maintenance of partition.

The new education and welfare reforms applied equally to nationalists as to unionists so Brooke's 1950s government felt nationalists would soon discover on what side their bread was buttered and the issue of the border would diminish. Instead the issue of the treatment of Mater Hospital soured the situation. A Roman Catholic foundation, the Mater sought to maintain its Catholic ethos by not coming under the control of the Hospitals Authority. The Unionist government said if it wanted to be independent so be it. The Mater would simply receive no government funding and would indeed have to go it alone. So, nationalists developed an attitude of wariness and distrust of how the reforms were being implemented. They suspected and expected discrimination and all social and educational arrangements of the 1950s came to be scrutinised carefully.

1950s education at primary and secondary levels continued along segregated lines. Roman Catholic schools unlike those of the other Christian denominations did not enter the state system post-war but were grant aided and remained under the control of the Roman Catholic authorities. At third level the one university, Queen's, was integrated but in terms of the teacher training colleges the Roman Catholic Church had opted to run its own colleges of St Mary's and St Joseph's alongside the state supported Stranmillis.

When, on Easter Monday 1949, the government of Eire declared an Irish Republic Brooke took the opportunity to squeeze a major concession from Attlee the Prime Minister and leader of the largely anti-partition Labour party. This was a new Ireland Act [June 1949] which contained a clause which came to be known as "The Guarantee". This clause stated that Northern Ireland would remain part of the United Kingdom until the government of Northern Ireland decided otherwise. Since that government was unionist dominated partition from the rest of Ireland seemed to be copper-fastened for long into the foreseeable future. The unionists were further reassured when their allies the Conservatives won the 1951 general election – Ulster was and would remain British!

How the issue of the border was dealt with in the 1950s is interesting. Governments in the newly declared Irish Republic took the view that nothing could be gained in terms of Irish unity by belligerence or violence. During the 1950s proposals were floated by southern politicians about reaching agreement on a federal structure for Ireland. They ran aground on unionist determination not to yield an inch.

The IRA was diametrically opposed to the "softly, softly" approach of successive southern governments. It still held that force was the only thing the British authorities understood. It regrouped and in 1956 launched a vicious border campaign. It was joined by another dissident republican splinter group Saor Uladh. Their violent campaign was ultimately doomed to failure.

The IRA's tactics had not advanced beyond those of the flying columns of the 1920s. It weakened its own impact by restricting the campaign to isolated RUC stations and Customs posts in border areas and in not targeting Belfast. The campaign also lacked popular support among the nationalist population both north and south. In 1957 de Valera, himself a survivor of the Easter Rising and a former IRA commander, actually ordered the round up of IRA suspects and introduced internment. This move together with effective work by the British army and RUC in the north ended with the campaign fizzling out.

Arguably a bigger challenge for the Stormont government than the IRA was the continued worsening of the economic situation in 1950s Northern Ireland. Jobs in traditional industries were bleeding away.

By 1958 there were 50,000 job losses with the highest percentage being in the traditional heavy industries and linen. Northern Ireland was a UK industrial black spot. People began to emigrate.

What could be done? A report for the Northern Ireland government published in 1955 highlighted many problems amongst which were:

- importing fuel and raw materials cost a fortune
- the transport infrastructure was woeful and left Northern Ireland struggling to connect to the mainland and other markets.
- many locally owned Northern Ireland firms were reluctant to move with the times and introduce new practices

even the climate was wrong!

The Ministry of Commerce [NI] worked hard to try to counter

this downward dynamic. It set up fully serviced factory premises to be leased by new firms and tried with some success to attract new industries to the province. Grants were made available to existing industries to update machinery and plant and to offset the cost of importing fuel. Nationalists noted cynically that only 10% of the new jobs went "west of the Bann" and cried discrimination. But to be fair, the lack of good transport infrastructure did not encourage new firms to move far out of range of the port of Belfast.

Brooke's government throughout the 1950s tried to pressure the Westminster government into declaring Northern Ireland an area of special economic concern and argued consistently for a higher subsidy to be paid to it out of the national purse. But nothing seemed able to halt the downward economic decline. One would have thought that the working class would have awoken to its fate much sooner and that growing concern for this loss of industry and jobs would have led to a growth of support for the Northern Ireland Labour Party and the trade unions. But in the minds of the Protestant working class socialism and trade unionism were irrevocably linked to anti-partitionism. The Protestant working class only registered its unease with traditional squiracy unionism by occasionally electing independent unionists such as Tommy Henderson or Norman Porter [both deemed to be more in touch with the needs of their Belfast working class constituents than other unionists].

At local level the Belfast Corporation reflected the political make up of the Stormont parliament.

Having the biggest urban population in the province it had to deal with the same social and economic problems presented to the regional government. Belfast Corporation consisted of Councillors and Aldermen. A new local government act in 1948 had greatly increased the responsibilities of the Corporation. It had responsibility among other things for education, public health, graveyards, parks, transport, library services, sewerage, sanitation, street cleaning and lighting, rubbish collection, a fire service, building social housing, buying land, planning and local roads! Money to pay for all of this was raised from local rates, government grants and revenue gained from providing services. A revaluation of property in Belfast in 1957 may have provided the addition of much needed funds to the public coffers but also raised a storm of protest from city centre businesses and shops.

Besides its other responsibilities Belfast Corporation encountered additional expenses because it was the only local government to actually own and maintain a Zoo and pleasure grounds!

Post war, housing shortage was a big problem and solving it set the Belfast Corporation Housing Department a huge challenge. Thirty-two percent of the urban-dwelling population of Northern Ireland lived in Belfast.

Between slum housing and bombed there were simply not enough houses to meet the demand. The council resisted expanding the city boundary so early attempts to solve the pressure saw the introduction of prefabs and experiments with high-rise flats.

The 1950s saw the beginnings of the new housing estates built on the fringe of the city boundary – Andersonstown, Newtownabbey, Dunmurray, Castlereagh, Highfield,Ballymurphy, Clara Park, Taughmonagh, Whiterock, Braniel, Mount Vernon and the list goes on. Desperate measures were taken by those wanting to get on to Council and Housing Trust lists.

Some of these measures involved doctors who by virtue of the newly introduced Health Service were now freely available to a public who previously had to rely on paying dispensary doctors.

A letter saying a member of the family was in danger of contracting TB would further the cause of getting housing applicants moved further up the list. Desperate people took desperate measures to obtain such a letter.

Welfare and health problems in Belfast were also acute. When the evacuated of Belfast had pitched up in Lisburn after the April Blitz of 1941 the Lisburn people had been appalled at the unwashed, undernourished, and unhealthy state of some of the evacuees. Not much had changed in the intervening years for the poor of the city. TB was a killer disease. In 1950 alone 524 in the province died from it. Figures for other causes of death add to the story of the poor health of the population of Northern Ireland. Cancer deaths were 2091 and death from heart disease 5037. According to the 1951 census, there were 667,821 men in Northern Ireland of whom only 3.1% were over the age of 75 and 703,112 women of whom 3.7% were aged 75 or over.

Traditional industries were in decline and this led to steady bouts of unemployment in Belfast. On all these things the Welfare State and Health Service would have a tremendous impact.

The standard of living of Belfast people would rise in the 1950s but the region as a whole would remain one of the most deprived in the U.K.

The children born in the 1950s were to be educated for a selective system and, if successful in passing the necessary exams, state sponsored through to university level. For the first time a significant group of working -class Protestant and Roman Catholic children could obtain a university degree. From this generation would emerge the politicised students and young adults of 1968 and some would step forward to give articulate voice to the long held social, economic and above all political grievances of their social groups.

In the rich tapestried backdrop to 1950s Belfast other events are shaking things up too. There is a war on somewhere, indeed there are several wars and violent disturbances going on at once.

A Cold War, tension in Berlin, a full scale war in Korea and troubles in Palestine, the Malay States and Egypt. The Chinese are growling away at everybody. The French are being attacked in their then colony of Vietnam by bicycle bombers. Several African states notably Kenya are in a state of revolt against British rule.

In the foreground of all of this Northern Ireland must have seemed like a quiet backwater of the Empire. Stormont was left to get on with it. The Imperial government at Westminster was too distracted by big problems on the world stage to keep its eye on us. "Benevolent neglect" is how their policy on Northern Ireland has been described.

But as the last minutes of 31st December 1949 ticked away the usual throng of revellers gathered in Custom House Square and round the Albert Clock to welcome in 1950 was not focussed on these things. Belfast had survived the war and though grim, grey and full of bombsites had much to be hopeful about in the promises held out by the new education system, Welfare State and Health Service.

CHAPTER 2

THE DECADE BEGINS

1950 GOT OFF TO an actual big bang. Three unlikely safe breakers had hi-jacked a Wolsey car and taking gelignite and detonators with them [obtained where?] set off to blow up a factory safe which they believed had a firm's wages in it. The whole enterprise though elaborately planned turned out badly. The inept robbers succeeded in blowing up the safe but it contained not a jot of cash. On the way out one robber not wishing the night to be a complete loss, stole a pair of water boots. These really high class thieves then drove to Banbridge stole another car to cover their tracks and driving on to Marino Halt took the bus home complete with the stolen water boots.

The RUC had a round up of usual suspects and when it was put to one of the thieves that his trousers resembled material found at the scene he confessed all and turned the other two in. They admitted breaking and entering, safe cracking and destruction of property but, indignantly issuing disclaimers, took the high moral ground over the theft of the water boots.

Meanwhile law abiding citizens of Belfast were determined to enjoy what was left of the Christmas/New Year holiday.

In the opening days of 1950 Belfast people flocked to post-Christmas entertainments. No wonder when one looks at the radio programming from "Auntie" BBC at prime time on 3rd January:

The Home Service 6.45pm - Bernie McCann[sings]. Edwin Rushe and partner [hand bells] and Gordon Howard [Banjo]

The Light Programme 6. 45pm -"Dick Barton".

What would you choose- the hand bells and banjo or the excitement of a radio private detective mystery with the racy opening music? No contest really!

Showing in Belfast in January 1950 were two professional Pantomimes, a host of amateur ones and a circus- "the greatest ever seen in Ireland". Betty Staff's, the other dance studios and halls were in full swing attracting those who wanted to quickstep.......... until the buses went off.

Belfast had lots of cinemas at the start of the '50s so that January aficionados of "the pictures" were spoilt for choice. They could do worse than to head for "The Imperial" where Bob Hope and Jane Russell were appearing in the comedy film, "The Paleface" or to the glitzy "Ritz" where you could sing and tap along with Judy Garland and Van Johnston in "The Good Old Summertime" [not very seasonal but Belfast, January 1950 was though mild,

A HOUSE PANTOMIME.—Tommy Morgan, as "Buttons," Powell, as "Cinders," in the ration book sketch from "rella," which is running at the Opera House.

very wet and a bit of artificial Hollywood sun did no harm]

The Opera House Panto',"Cinderella" described by the press reviewers as, "a glittering success and with a big cast", was playing to packed houses.

There were 750 unreserved seats for every performance at 1/6d each. The reserved seating was more expensive with prices ranging from 6/= to 2/6d. A rival panto, "Babes in the Woods" showing at "The Empire", was also a sell out each night

Playing to enthusiastic crowds at "The Royal Hippodrome "was "Dr. Hunter's Circus". It starred Captain Rossi and his lions who left the audience

breathless with excitement as he carried out his "unbelievable feats" whilst at the same time "fondling his savage companions"!

There were chimps, a giant python, Hindu dancers and Madame Truzzi with her "magnetic personality", poodles and ponies. All this entertainment and exotica coupled with the fact that The Ministry of Food announced on 3rd January that tins of that tasteless and offensively grey coloured fish Snoek plus Pork Brawn, Sausages in Brine and Macaroni Casserole with Pork in Tomato Sauce had all just come off ration must have produced a feeling of near euphoria in the citizens of Belfast facing the new decade.

There was nobody sitting glued to the television.

Television did not arrive in Northern Ireland until 1953, just in time for The Coronation which was broadcast in June of that year. However as early as 5th January 1950 the local papers reported on the impact of a rumour sweeping Belfast that T.V. transmissions broadcast from the receiver in Sutton Coalfield in England could be picked up here. Why order a new radio when you could spend your cash on a bang up to date T.V. set? Alarmed radio dealers found orders for radios being cancelled. One enterprising dealer, Mr. Kelso, decided on affirmative action. He brought in testing equipment and erected, in his own back garden, a 45ft mast. He then called a press conference. Reporters crowding into his home were shown a TV screen fuzzy with static. No pictures only a dim flicker of something was seen during 15 minutes of observation and dial twiddling. Could the fuzzy picture be caused by the effect of trolley buses passing on the nearby road asked a sceptical press?

To hammer home his point that TV was a no go Mr Kelso then hauled all the equipment and the mast to the top of the Horseshoe Road the next day. Same experiment: same result.

A triumphant Mr. Kelso told the press, "few people in Belfast will want a Television set which has to be operated halfway up a mountain." His coup de grace was, "In any case the Post Office does not issue T.V. licences for Northern Ireland". [Belfast Newsletter 5/1/50].

But look out cinema, TV is on its way and by 3rd January of the next year classes for Television Engineers are being formed at the Marine Radio College, 2 Eglantine Avenue, Belfast

But first things first, what was 1950s Belfast like?

CHAPTER 3

BACK-TO-BACKS AND COBBLESTONES

IN COMPARISON WITH TODAY'S city it was like a different planet. At the start of the 1950s Belfast was a city in which nineteenth century stabling was gradually being turned into garages and the keeping of pigs in yards was being discouraged. There were horse drawn vehicles still in abundance to hold up the traffic - coal carts, fruiterers' carts, haulage carts, rag and bone men, men selling steaming coal-brick. There were horse troughs and instructions on walls at steep hills for carters to get down and walk their horses slowly up. A blacksmith still worked in the heart of the city. Occasionally the knife grinder or pot repairer would appear in a street or even a roundabout pulled by a little horse; small children took their places on the colourful seats and were whirled about by hand.

It was still a city of densely packed streets of terraced houses with half moons scubbed on the pavement outside the front doors, gleaming lino in the halls and tin baths hung from a nail in the whitewashed back yards. Outside toilets in the yard were the norm in these houses and under beds could be found a "gussunder" [chamber pot]. Each house had a "gloryhole" under the stairs where sundries like the ironing board resided.

IMPORTANT NOTICE

Owing to the drastic reduction ordered by the Government in the allocation of ingredients used in the manufacture of **ORMO Fancy Bread and Biscuits,** we are reluctantly compelled to reduce substantially our present output of these varieties.

In accordance with the policy of the Company NO SUBSTITUTE INGREDIENTS are used in the manufacture of Ormo Products.

We regret the inconvenience to our customers and would ask their kind indulgence during this difficult period. We hope they will appreciate that our inability to supply their requirements is due entirely to circumstances beyond our control and would assure them that everything possible will be done to arrange equitable distribution of the limited quantities available.

Vans in all districts.   'Phone 41241 (4 lines).

ORMEAU BAKERY LTD., BELFAST

By the end of the decade the small black ranges regularly polished with "Zebo" would be replaced with the latest "Devon Grate with all – night burner" and people were looking to move to new Corporation housing with inside plumbing.

The milkman delivered pint glass bottles of milk to the doorstep – even on Christmas Day. There were bread rounds-men doing weekly orders for big loaves, barn bracks, Paris buns and Iced Diamonds. The housewives clustered at the back of the bread van while a seemingly endless tray of bread products was pulled from it. Belfast, probably the only place in the world where even today you can get a choice of brown or white lemonade also had its lemonade delivered to the doorstep.

Children played on the streets or in their gardens from they came home from school until darkness fell. Then the litany of names began, calling them in for bed; no-one seemed too fussed about "stranger danger". It seemed that the worst that could happen was a telling off from a neighbour for too boisterous play or the invasion of your patch by a hostile gang of children from the next street. Traffic was light in the side streets and there were usually no cars parked outside front doors. Any vehicles about had to rattle over cobblestones in side streets though main roads were tarmaced.

By the mid-'50s new electric standards were replacing the old gas lighting on the Castlereagh Road. But, until the completion of the scheme throughout the city much of Belfast at dusk still saw the arrival of the lamplighter lighting the gas lamps. These would bathe the streets in pools of dull yellow light which had the effect of emphasising a sort of secret darkness beyond it.

All during the '50s cattle were still driven through Belfast to sales yards and the abattoir. One young heifer actually ran wild through the city centre after escaping from a sales yard in Oxford Street.

It had quite a scamper. First it made for the grounds of "Inst" then it about turned and jumped a 3 ft high wall into the grounds of the City Hall from Donegall Square East and belted towards the Garden of Remembrance!

Watched by a crowd of over 200 the drovers used an old trick and drove six other cattle into the grounds. On seeing companions the heifer calmed herself and was finally captured. Her fate? She was shipped to England for slaughter.

Belfast by the close of the decade was a more prosperous city than at the beginning. With the benefit of Hire Purchase and the wider selection of consumer products on offer, a family could transform its life. "Cyril Lord Carpets" boasted that a whole room 12ft x9ft could be carpeted for just £16 in "rich deep-pile non-fade colours". The carpet backed by latex could furthermore be cut and laid by the householder. Who could resist?

The decade started with food rationing but from the mid-'50s onwards those returning to Belfast noticed that people actually had enough money to eat out. The same Cyril Lord of the carpets fame had brought Belfast the new Thompson's Restaurant with a "different eating experience" on each floor.

Car ownership had increased giving the Corporation sore heads trying to sort out congestion black spots such as around the City Hall, Queen's Bridge and Bradbury Place.

But all things are relative. In May 1958 an NSPCC Inspector submitted a report on a family consisting of a mother and seven children. They were living in appalling Dickensian circumstances. They had no heat, electricity or food. The children had neither shoes nor socks and only the clothes they stood up in. The family had no beds, crockery or cutlery and had been reduced to drinking out of jam jars.

The city continued to have an amazing array of department stores and even added to them with the arrival of the new "C&A" in Donegall Place. This purpose built store had been erected on a bombsite which up to that point had been a car park. It had 17,000 square feet of showroom space over three floors. On the ground floor you would find millinery, knitwear, skirts and blouses. The first floor housed the coat department and children's wear and the second floor was given over totally to dresses.

Soon a Men's Wear department was opened advertising "high quality at low prices" –

"For the man on his way to the top –a well cut rayon and nylon two-piece suit in popular charcoal grey. Self supporting trousers. Regular fittings - £5-19-0."

One wonders about those trousers and the wisdom of standing too near a naked flame in that suit!

The Co-operative Stores in York Street with its "Co -Quarter" and "Dividend" was a favourite with everybody. I can hardly remember my telephone number but know like an awful lot of people over a certain age the "Divi" number. Ours was 91304 and was given every time a purchase of any kind was made in a "Co" shop.

In Royal Avenue there was a plethora of stores to choose from ranging from Gents' and Ladies' outfitters to general outfitters and haberdashery. These included D. Lyle Hall & Sons, Mc Williams and Archer, Newell's, the new Goorwitch's and then the gleaming art deco Sinclair's with its big clock at the top of its stepped front. On up towards Donegall Place was the Swiss Arcade and Jean Millar's Bridal Wear and a short step away in North Street the "35/= Tailor's" plus Warnock's and Magee's. Even bigger stores were in Castle Place and Donegall Place.

The Bank Buildings occupied the store now used by Primark and on the opposite corner of Castle Place and Donegall Place stood Anderson and McAuley's the first store in Belfast to have an escalator installed. Children were brought in especially to have a go on it and children also loved the window decorations in this shop at Christmas. It sold everything from embroidery thread to suites of furniture. Christmas 1959 saw the biggest spending spree of the decade and the store tried to entice customers to buy Irish Linen goods by introducing a gimmick – "The Lucky Linen Leprechaun". Customers fortunate enough to encounter the "Leprechaun" would find themselves being handed the Anderson and McAuley equivalent of a pot of gold – a linen cheque! But, a rigmarole had to be gone through by the customer on sentry-go for the approach of the "Leprechaun".

When the "Leprechaun" stopped you it would say, "Excuse me, do you know Irish linen makes wonderful giving?" To which the customer had to reply, "Yes. And wonderful living too and here's my receipt to prove it." If one word of the reply was wrong the "Leprechaun" was not obliged to cough up.

In an area which ran from Castle Place to Lombard Street stood Robb's and not far away in High Street a furriers- Swears and Wells- Francis Curley Ltd., Cochrane's, Spackman's and Woolworth's. Robb's was another big store which sold everything and was a big rival to the "Co" in the Santa's Grotto stakes at Christmas. In High Street was the newly opened Arnott's. Again built on a former bomb site this store advertised itself as "a shopper's paradise". The store featured the latest in modern design including dropped ceilings, strip lighting and central heating.

Many shops in Belfast at that time had a system of dealing with payments, receipts and change. When an item was purchased the assistant would put the cash into a metal tube and screw on a lid. The tube was then inserted into another opening in the wall and at lightning speed sucked away by pneumatic force into the unknown region of the cashier's office

Tubes with receipts and correct change would then whizz back along the same route. Wary small children refused to stand anywhere near the openings in case they too would be sucked away and receipted.

The new premises for C. & A. Modes, Ltd., at Donegall Place, Belfast, which will be opened today.

At the top of Donegall Place stood Brand's and Norman's Arcade. On the opposite side now occupied by Marks and Spencer's stood the brand new C &A and the jewel in the architectural crown of the big shops, Robinson and Cleaver's. The best view of this building is still from the grounds of the City Hall opposite. It is a wonderful pile of six storeys crowned with copper domes.

It billed itself as "The Royal Irish Linen House" and around its exterior on the first floor were sculpted the heads of many of its royal and important patrons including George Washington [representing America], Queen Victoria and Prince Albert and the gloriously named Maharajah of Cooch-Bihar. There are also other figures representing Australia and Canada. Looking upwards towards the third floor the observer can see cherubs holding symbols to do with linen and flax.

The interior did not disappoint either. Robinson and Cleaver's had a fabulous staircase of gleaming white Sicilian marble the like of which would have done justice to a chateau on the Loire.

In contrast to the luxury of Robinson and Cleaver's was the shopping experience of another kind offered by the old Smithfield Market which could be accessed from Garfield Street.

This was a higgelty-piggelty of one storey shops and stalls under a glass roof; a veritable Aladdin's cave of treasures old and new, used and resold, unloved and desired.

Here and in the surrounding streets you could buy an eclectic array of goods from second -hand books, furniture, electronics, hardware, records and clothes. There was McQuillan's ["this is a walk through shop"], Hugh Greer's, Havelin's ["Any type of lock repaired"], Jay's Records,

FASHION SHOWS IN BELFAST

This attractive suit was one of the many autumn fashions displayed at the Belfast Co-operative Society yesterday.

Shearer's, McCusker's, Lily McDowell's, and Kavanagh's ["I buy anything"] to name but a few of the favourites. In nearby Garfield Street stood a shop beloved of children - "Birdseed" Creighton's Pet Shop.

Even by the end of the '50s Belfast still had its big firms too. Mackie's made a fair share of all the world's leaf-fibre preparing and spinning machinery, the Ropeworks at Connswater supplied the world with ropes, twines, netting cords, baler twine, sash cords and fishing nets. The Sirocco Works, set over 12 acres and employing 1500, made 60% of all machinery used in the world for the drying and processing of tea leaves as well as fans extracting dust, steam and vapour. Harland and Wolff still had the greatest output of any British shipyard.

The 8,700ton cargo vessel, "Elmbank" was the last launch of the decade. But the ship building industry in the city was in a serious crisis which would come to a head in the sixties. Outmoded practices, delivery dates not met, penalties incurred as a result and strikes would

all contribute to its steady demise. Rising manufacturing centres elsewhere in Europe and in the Far East and new man-made materials would gradually threaten the rest of Belfast's industries.

Belfast's fate would be not to adjust quickly enough and then to be plunged into decades of political and civil strife.

The man in the street in Belfast could not see any of this coming.

For the ordinary citizens of Belfast life would slowly improve during the 1950s.

Rationing would be left behind and as the decade went on there would be more money to spend and more to spend it on, new holiday destinations, and perhaps a TV or a car to aspire to.

Those short on money could still be consumers by courtesy of Hire Purchase, Provident Cheque, the "Co Quarter", Christmas clubs, grocery clubs and shoe clubs.

When the '50s ended Belfast people had had over a decade of the new system of welfare, state benefits and the Health Service. New schools had been built and new housing estates developed. The unionists on Belfast Corporation and at Stormont felt pleased with themselves. After all there was no such level of prosperity or benefit in the Irish Republic. Partition for unionists was justified and must be maintained. Surely nothing could upset this applecart?

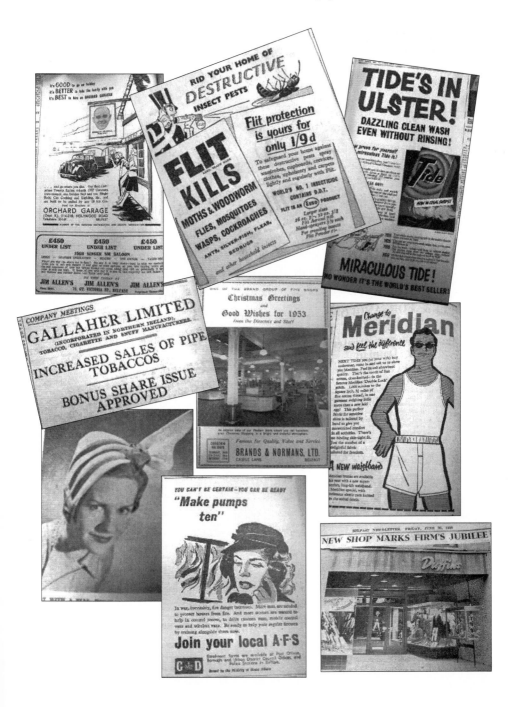

CHAPTER 4

SCHOOL

THE EDUCATION ACT NORTHERN Ireland 1947 followed the same principles as the Butler Act for England and Wales but with some provision for local circumstances.

It raised the school leaving age from 14 to 15 and made provision for a scholarship exam – the 11+ or "Qually" to be taken at the age of 11. This exam opened up the chance of a grammar school education to many 100s of children whose parents would not otherwise have been able to afford it. It also set a considerable challenge for the existing school provision. The existing grammar schools in particular would find it hard to accommodate a big influx of new pupils. Before the war in Northern Ireland as a whole only 20% of the children aged 11+ actually had won scholarship places to the grammar schools. The remaining 80% had been faced with a choice. If parents could afford it they could buy their child a place at a grammar school if not, the child transferred to the local Secondary Intermediate.

In Belfast it fell to the Belfast Education Authority and the Roman Catholic Authorities to try to sort out the problem for the city's children. It was pure guess work trying to calculate how many children would pass the new exam and how many free grammar school places would have to be provided. Not all those who passed would choose to avail themselves of a grammar school place: some would prefer the "Tech" or the local Secondary Intermediate. The Belfast Education Authority [B.E.A.] tried to predict the increased need with a handy formula = all existing pupils +two children per new house + 1 child each new flat.

Simple as it was the formula would not work. There was a falling birth rate in Belfast and many families seeking better housing gradually moved out beyond the existing city boundary to new estates and other education authority areas. There really was no effective way of forecasting the number of children needing Primary, Secondary, Grammar and Technical school places. So, the B.E.A. had to do its calculation on the hoof each year.

In the light of the current debate about the merits/ demerits of the 11+ system of selection it is interesting to note that throughout the period of its introduction grave reservation was expressed by many individuals about the efficacy of this test.

McNeilly in his book about the early work of the Belfast Education Authority: "Exactly Fifty Years" expresses this opinion about the 11+ test:

".....the new test was not an examination, or even had the appearance of one. In practical operation it was, in essence, little different from the grading of cattle or pigs, but with fewer dependable criteria."

Belfast Education Authority faced with implementing the exam wrote to the Minister of Education suggesting that performance in the 11+ should not be the automatic key to a grammar school place. It wanted the test to be supplemented by two further tests and an interview! The Ministry of Education was immovable. The Authority in the first years of the test anticipated being flooded with a tsunami of qualified pupils claiming their grammar school places.

Remember, before the 11+ was introduced into Northern Ireland 265 pupils had sat scholarship exams and entered the grammar sector. Usually about 200 made it each year [20%].

In the first year of the introduction of the 11+ 4764 pupils in the province sat the exam and 2104 passed [41%]!

As Northern Ireland had a segregated system, costs of maintaining the Roman Catholic schools fell between the Roman Catholic Church and the Northern Ireland Ministry of Education but a vista of expense

A Cat has nine lives—You have one—was the title of the talk on Road Safety given by Mr. E. Strathdee (hon. secretary, Belfast Safety Council) to pupils of Jaffe Primary School, Cliftonville Road, yesterday. He was assisted by Miss Iris Shawyer (who plays Dick Whittington's cat in the pantomime on Ice at the Opera House) and Patrolman J. Cunningham.

now opened before the **B**elfast **E**ducation **A**uthority, the biggest in the province in providing for the pupils under its control. More money would have to be found for new schools, the extension of existing ones, clothing grants, maintenance grants, travel grants, school meals.

Besides the problems caused by the new test the B.E.A. had other school related issues to deal with.

What was the provision for those who did not pass the 11+ or, though qualifying, did not wish to take up a Grammar school place? What about those children with special education needs or disabilities? What state was the Primary sector in; was it geared up to preparing children for the new exam?

The alternative to Grammar school was the Secondary Intermediate. The rise in the school leaving age and the demands of modern technology would necessitate the building of new Intermediates and the modernisation of others. Once in an Intermediate a pupil would find him/herself subject to the same demands as the grammar school pupil with regard to uniform, behaviour and manners and would be in the first two years given quite a rigorous academic education. The difference between this and the Grammar was only in the choice of subjects offered in the curriculum. Grammar school pupils were afflicted by having to learn Latin and perhaps Greek, and a second Modern Language was offered. Rarely was a subject like Technology offered to a Grammar school child and no girl in a Grammar school ever did anything vaguely associated with secretarial work. The nearest they got to "hands-on" was Domestic Science.

On 21st March 1954 "The Belfast Newsletter in its column "Woman's View" carried a little piece on "Careers Advice for Girls" perhaps aimed at the bright girls in the Intermediate. It highlights the importance for girls of staying in the academic stream of the intermediate and combining that with a good commercial course as well. Girls are advised to get a good education and aim for Senior Certificate as there was a shortage of well educated secretaries. It fails to point out that in the '50s when the well educated secretary married she could expect to lose her job.

Nursery provision was poor and generally situated in areas of social deprivation. In 1950 under the control of the B.E.A. were nursery schools like Edenderry in Sydney Street West, Arellian [founded by the Old Girls' of Richmond Lodge] in Utility Street, McArthur in Church Street East, Forthriver, Frederick Street and Jennymount. The

Authority took over two further schools which had been run by mills, Owen O'Cork on the Beersbridge Road and Tudor Lodge once owned by Ewart's Mill. By 1959 only 310 children had Nursery school places.

Children below the school age of 5 years old were more likely to be accommodated in an existing primary school in classes endearingly titled Junior and Senior Infants. In my primary school on one ill judged occasion Senior Infants were left in charge of Juniors while the teacher left the room.

She returned to a scene of chaos and howling Seniors. The Juniors had run amok and the Seniors had lost control and then the run of themselves. Lots of sitting with the arms folded and then fingers on lips followed that day.

ROAD SAFETY CINEMA SHOWS—All eyes on the screen of the mobile cinema in Templemore Street on Saturday, when, in conjunction with the Belfast Safety Council, a show lasting 45 minutes was presented. The van, which has been touring Ulster, gave eight shows in various parts of the city.

Primary schools were a mixture of Education Authority schools, church schools and old mill schools. The schools were not all in a good state of repair and, in many, more than one class was taught in the one big room. When class A had its weekly "Singing Together" lesson Class B across the room had to engage in silent reading or copying from the blackboard! Heating was a bit hit and miss and older primaries had outside toilets. A few of the oldest even had multiple seaters where three or four children could be seated side by side!

In a classroom there might be a piano, a nature table, a blackboard but, until the mid '50s, no radio or T.V. If bored with vulgar fractions children could look at the walls of classrooms festooned with maps of the Empire still showing places to stir the imagination like Beutshuanaland and Tanganika.

Primary school children were not a healthy lot. They suffered intermittently from outbreaks of nits, impetigo, measles, mumps, scarlet fever, ringworm. There was a terror of diphtheria and worse - polio. Those with eye problems sported the fetching look of pink or blue round rimmed glasses with a patch over the problem eye. Those with shorn locks because of nits wore a woollen hat in class like those favoured by today's boy rappers. Boys wore short trousers until they were teenagers, girls suffered their hair to be nightly screwed around pipe cleaners to produce what their mothers hoped were pretty ringlets like the girl in the Pears' soap advert. Any girl despaired off as having pipe -cleaner -resistant -straight as a plumb line -hair had it bobbed [if they were lucky by a hair dresser] and sported a "donkey fringe" and large nodding bow to hold back the most recalcitrant strands.

The 1950s were also littered with stammering youngsters. Picture then the consternation of mothers when they read what Miss Marion Fleming, Vice-Principal of the National School of Speech Therapy was reported as saying two days into the new decade about stammering She gave the contributory causes as quarrelling parents, over-mothering, physical defects about which the child was sensitive and drunken parents. Can't you just see every mother of a stammering child queuing up ready to "do" her?

Children dealt sanguinely with the regular visits by the school nurse. She invariably tore strips off anyone without clean hair, hands, nails or hankies. Those given to wiping runny noses on cardigan sleeves were practically taken out and flogged.

Speaking of which, corporal punishment of all for **any** misdemeanour was the norm. Children were used to the spectacle of someone hauled out in front of the class to be given "six of the best" across the hands or bottom or with having to duck as a blackboard duster screamed down the room in the direction of a day-dreamer. Punishable offences ranged from having no home work to getting **anything** wrong. Looking crooked at a teacher on a bad day could land even the best in bother!

Play space at the school was often limited to a small yard where the children played a mixture of Tig, skipping, "Chasies" [this just involved running after each other like maniacs], Hopscotch if there was chalk to draw up the grid and space to play and throwing and catching ball games.

At the end of Break or Lunch time a teacher would appear blow a whistle or ring a hand bell and as in the morning, everyone would line up in their class sets and march back indoors.

Class sizes gave cause for concern. Most classes had over 38 pupils in them: up to 50 was not unusual. It would take the building of new schools, the closure of the least repairable, the takeover of the

Protestant church schools and the training of many new teachers to bring these numbers down to an acceptable figure.

By 1958-59 progress had been made and the teacher/pupil ratio in Primaries was down on average to 1/38

E.S.N/S.E.N. - there is more than a simple rearrangement of letters here. There is a chasm of perception, strategy and provision between the educational provision made in the 1950s and that made in the opening of the 21st Century for children with special needs or disabilities.

Children with special needs or disabilities [Educationally Sub-Normal] were in the parlance of the '50s referred to as "sub-normal" or as "spastics." and even then those called "spastics" were divided into "educatable" and "non-educatable". There was only marginal integration of S.E.N. children into mainstream education. In Harding Memorial the B.E.A. experimented with a unit for the hearing impaired but only in order to free up space in The Deaf and Dumb Institute! No wonder the mother of one partially hearing child determined to avoid segregation on grounds of disability swore the child to secrecy about her hearing impairment. The child always collared a seat at the front of the room.

It was not unusual for a pupil with learning difficulties to remain in primary education long after his/her peers had progressed to secondary level. Faced with a big class to control it would take a very enlightened teacher to accommodate the needs of all the pupils plus such a one. In my P.4. class there was a big 14 year old who did not speak and who was very useful turning the skipping rope for us at lunchtime in the playground. He spent his day drawing, and playing with plasticine. We did not mind him and he was too big to be bullied.

Then there was the problem of how school children were to be fed. Very few schools had kitchens, dining halls and serveries. The decision was taken to mass produce school dinners at central kitchens such as Park Parade, Strandtown, Everton, Graymount. These mass produced meals would then be delivered to the schools and only require reheating. It is worth noting and may explain the dining experience of school children of the '50s that food rationing continued until 1954 and the recipes of the meals kitchens were based on those of the wartime British Restaurants which specialised in the bulk produce of food made with the cheapest of ingredients.

Put together any group of those who took school dinners in the '50s and they will remember "frog's spawn" [Tapioca], stew with very dodgy gristly bits of grey meat, stodgy cake and custard, thin watery soup, lumpy mashed potato resembling wall paper paste and the all pervading smell of cabbage.

To obtain one of these great school meals a pupil bought a roll of green dinner tickets for the week. Those who qualified for free school meals were issued with a ticket of a different colour. They might as well have been handed Stars of David to wear! All tickets were handed over in public so it was dead easy to pick out the free dinner gang.

No old nonsense about damaging pupil self-esteem or stigmatising people in those days!

It was things like the different colour of dinner ticket which put off many who passed "the Qually" from going into a Grammar school with all its added expense. All pupils at Secondary level and some at Primary level wore a school uniform which had to be purchased from designated retailers in Belfast who, with a virtual monopoly, could charge through the nose. Clothing grants were available for struggling families but were rigorously means tested.

The August newspapers each year in the '50s carry many advertisements from an array of outfitters advertising everything the well equipped pupil could need for "Back to School". A glimpse shows the expense with which parents of working class children could be faced.

Everybody had to have a schoolbag. Morrison's of North Street was selling cowhide schoolbags with weatherproof flaps at *32/6.The alternative cheaper canvas schoolbags were still dear at 10/9. Average prices for other essentials were:

- School pullovers 23/= [any mother who could knit bought the wool and set to knitting school jumpers and cardigans as this was cheaper than paying the outfitters prices for the designated school pullover].

- Gabardine coats [Navy or Bottle] retail at 89/6 and schools insisted on this outdoor coat.
- Blazers sold from 32/6 but sometimes this expense could be avoided by buying the gabardine and having a school jumper for indoors.
- Everybody had to have the necessary sports gear too. Rugby boots cost between 28/6 and 50/= and Hockey Sticks from 19/= to 35/=. Football boots retailed from 16/6 to 25/=
- Headgear- school caps for boys and berets for girls emblazoned with the school badge were worn to and from school until the pupil left.

[£1 in old money was 20shillings. [20/=] :1/= was 12 old pence [12d]: so 32/6 in today's money =£1.62p. This was about a third of a week's wages for some people.]*

Girls had also to obtain a variety of what could only be called heavy duty knickers in school colours. They were mortified to be seen in public wearing the special knickers reserved for gym and athletics. Boys smirkingly referred to the knickers as "Empire builders".

PHYSICAL EDUCATION DISPLAY AT ASHFIELD GRAMMAR SCHOOL—Grammar Intermediate school pupils who took part in the display in the school's new gymnasium night. The performance will be repeated to-night.

Then there was the milk ration - one third of a pint a day per child. In Primary school the milk was carried to the classrooms in crates by the Milk Monitors. Rarely was the milk cold.

In winter it was left beside a heater to thaw and in summer often in the sun until Break time.

In Primary school being a Milk Monitor was usually the second rung on the ladder of success. The first rung was being sent on "messages" or being designated Straw Monitor [giving out the drinking straws for the milk Milk Monitor] This was followed in the promotion stakes by

Ink Monitor- a responsible job filling the ink wells which were set into the desks. This was done by pouring the ink from a big jug into tiny ink wells.

It required a person with a steady hand and no malice against another member of the class [those with an axe to grind could have drowned an enemy in blue-black]. Ultimate progression to the top of the success ladder allowed a pupil to be sent for the teacher's cup of tea and biscuit at Break time.

The chosen on the ladder of success played for high stakes. They might be those with posh wooden pencil cases, their socks always pulled up to their knees, tens out of tens and smug looks on their faces but they risked the sneers of the rest of the class as "licks" or "toadies" or worse a duffing up in the playground.

In Secondary schools the system of getting your third of a pint was simpler. The milk was just set at one or two distribution points and it was a serve yourself system at Break. Often extra rations of biscuits could be bought from the school Tuck Shop. The elitism of Milk Monitors was thus avoided.

By 1955 Mr Midgeley, the Minister of Education, was able to take stock of how well the whole system was working.

Twenty-Five new schools had been built -18 Primary, 5 Secondary and 2 Grammar- and a further 15 Primary and 23 Secondary Intermediate were under construction. There is hardly a month goes by in the '50s when a newspaper does not feature a school opening, extension or a picture of buildings under construction. In comparison with the struggle to fund school buildings programmes nowadays it is a remarkable feat. The Minister estimated that by 1958 more than 50% of pupils aged 11+ would be in secondary schools fit for purpose.

NEW SCHOOL OPENED IN BELFAST

ASHFIELD (Boys')
Secondary Intermediate   A section of the new secondary intermediate school for boys at Ashfield

✳

CHAPTER 5

HOMES AND JOBS

First blocks of flats built by the Corporation

Official opening by Minister of Health

1951 WAS A CENSUS YEAR. In the debate about the census arrangements the Minister of Finance, Major Maynard Sinclair, urged Northern Ireland people to be honest. All replies to census questions he assured them would be treated in the strictest confidence. In particular people were urged to be honest about giving their age. Major Sinclair pointed out that in the 1937 Census the number of people giving their age as under 40, 50 or 60 was 50% higher than those giving their ages as 41+, 51+, or 61+ rendering Northern Ireland a sort of unrealistic pre -World War 2 Peter Pan land.

If people heeded the plea for honesty and the figures for the 1951 Census are accurate then this picture emerges. The total population of Northern Ireland was 1,370,933 [the Republic of Ireland was 2,958,878]. Of this population 32.3% - 443,680 lived in Belfast. The only comparable city in respect of size of population was Edinburgh with a population of 466,761.

In terms of the average number of people per square mile, Edinburgh had 9.225; Belfast has double that with 18.564. The Census of Production for Belfast given in "The Ulster Year Book 1950-53 " lists the following as the main industries: textiles, clothing, engineering, shipbuilding and repair, aircraft production, food, drink, and tobacco products

Two main problems therefore confronted the Stormont government and Belfast Corporation in the 1950s - how to best house this densely packed population and how to continue to provide work.

Housing

In 1951 on top of the thirty-two percent of the urban population of Northern Ireland living in Belfast a further seven percent lived around the boundary of the city. The norm was for the majority of people to rent their homes from private landlords, the Corporation or another social housing provider such as the Northern Ireland Housing Trust. The Blitz of 1941 had seriously destroyed and badly damaged housing stock particularly in the North and West of the city. The test was to replace these homes, clear slum dwellings and build even more new houses to meet a ravenous demand.

Housing available to the working class in the city was generally of a poor quality. There were streets upon streets of late nineteenth /early twentieth century mill houses – basically, terraced back to backs – "two up/two down". In these houses you could not swing the proverbial cat. Open the front door and you were confronted with a steep flight of stairs to the upper storey of two bedrooms. Opening a door to the left or right took you straight into the small living space with perhaps a small range for cooking or, if the family was a bit go- ahead, a Devon grate built into the fireplace. Off the living space was the scullery. It was only adequate enough for a small table, a gas stove, cupboard and Belfast sink.

A door opened from here to a tiny yard which held sometimes a mangle, tin bath hung up on a hook, the metal bin, the toilet and a lean- to for storing coal.

In a back to back the bin had to be carried through the house to be left on the street for collection. Many of these houses had not changed all that much since Dr. Hamilton, the city's Medical Officer in the nineteenth century had complained about their poor lack of sanitation, state of repair and dampness.

In some parts of the city there were still little courts of one storey cottage type dwellings - some with neither running water nor electricity!

Such was the pressure of population versus the supply of housing that there were also overcrowded large houses fallen on hard times, where families rented one room and used it for living and sleeping purposes and toilets were used in common by all residents. Cooking facilities in rented rooms were sadly inadequate with all cooking done over a gas ring or the open fire. It must have been hard to keep common areas like toilets clean. Another unsatisfactory situation was that young married couples unable to rent accommodation of their own had to move in with parents in perhaps already cramped houses.

What could be done to improve the housing stock?

In 1945 a planning commission had considered widening the city boundary but had decided against it. The post-war estimate was that 22,000 new homes had to be built to accommodate demand. Given the 1945 planning commission's decision this would have to be unrealistically done inside the existing boundary.

However by the beginning of the 1950s Belfast Corporation wisely took steps to acquire 525 acres of land beyond the boundary and marked it out for proposed estates. These would include Highfield, Ballymurphy, Clara Park, Mount Vernon, Inverary, Taughmonagh, Whiterock and Ashfield.

Slums and bombsites would also have to be cleared and Belfast people persuaded to consider living in pre-fabs, flats and maisonettes. The first 1000 prefabs were constructed and occupied by April 1950; by the end of the year 2000 had been set up not just in Belfast but right across Northern Ireland.

These were considered temporary homes until more permanent ones could be built. A good example would be Sunnyside Bungalows at the bottom of Sunnyside Street and Ormeau Embankment. Prefabs were built for £1925 each and rented out at 12/6 per week [this rose by 1959 to 15/- p.w.]. The bungalows at Sunnyside have been long demolished to give way to a private housing development. but, some of these "temporary" prefabs lasted, as at Taughmonagh, well into the last quarter of the twentieth century.

By then they were considered seriously inadequate as homes. What a contrast to how they were thought of in the 1950s. For those renting a room in a relative's house or living in damp, sub -standard mill houses they were seen as a paradise.

A prefab had a good size living room and two or three bedrooms, a bathroom with water heated by a back boiler grate and a system to circulate the hot air from the fire around the rooms. The kitchen had a gas cooker and - wonder of wonders - a gas fridge as standard. Outside there was a brick coal shed and a garden.

But, by '59 deterioration was appearing in the fabric of the bungalows. Tenants complained about the weather-proofing of doors and windows and that there was corrosion in chimneys and on roofs. The aluminium used to construct the prefabs was of a poor quality and it too was degrading. The Corporation had to press on with brick built dwellings.

It was thought that Belfast people would not take to living in flats and largely this was to be true of many. People liked their own space and even when transferred from old terrace houses to modern blocks of flats the housewife would treat the exterior walk way like a street and make sure she kept it swept. It was not unusual to see the familiar washed and bleached half moon outside each front door on a landing. However, flat dwellers were to miss the camaraderie of the street where on a summer's evening people would come out and lean against their window sills to have a conversation. In flats people went in and closed their doors and that was that. On 13th May 1952 the first block of flats built by the Corporation at Parkmount was opened by Dame Dehra Parker. Soon more flats were under construction at Skegoniel Avenue.

The Corporation did its best to make the new flats inviting. A typical example was Annadale Flats. Stormont Minister, Dame Dehra Parker again officiated at the opening in April 1953. These were three storey blocks consisting of two types which, determined by the position of the living room, were either two or three bed. All the living rooms had a south or west facing aspect which ensured they were bright.

Inside a block of flats was an entrance hall which served six flats with staircase access to two flats on each floor. Occupants proud of their new dwellings would devise a method of sharing the cleaning of this entrance way and the stairs. The ground floor flats had two bedrooms and those on the second and third storey had either two or three bedrooms. Each flat was equipped with a back boiler grate, fitted kitchen cupboards and a separate larder. There was a good bathroom and on the top two storeys the kitchen gave access to a small balcony on which there was a rubbish chute. The ground floor flats with their separate pram store were clearly intended for families with small children. Outside in the court yards between the blocks were the clothes drying lines.

Many schemes for Corporation flats followed the Annadale model.

In 1955 it was decided that since in 1954-55 alone 2500 applicants were still on the housing list that three ten storey blocks should be built at Annadale each block consisting of eighty flats. Thus the trend towards more high rises would follow in the late '50s and '60s and present ultimately the problems the Corporation sought to avoid in its well intentioned schemes of the early 1950s.

The newly established housing association, The Northern Ireland Housing Trust, went at the housing problem with a will. In the eleven months from 1st January 1951 to 3oth November 1952 it built 1608 houses and acquired 79 sites in which a further 16,000 homes could be built in the province. Nearing completion in Belfast by 1952 were Dundonald, Holywood and Suffolk estates. The association had bought land at Andersonstown and at the Braniel which the Trust was hoping to develop in two or three years time when services such as electricity, sewage disposal and mains water could be laid on.

By 1954 the Trust had forged ahead with estates at Rathcoole, Dunmurry, Dundonald, Graymount, Castlereagh, Suffolk, Whitewell, Cliftondene and Andersonstown and work on the Braniel had begun. In 1955 it purchased 400 acres of land bounded by the River Lagan and Newtownbreda Road and once part of Lord Deramore's land to build its new Belvoir Park estate.

It was estimated that by the middle of 1952 one in every forty-two people in Northern Ireland was living in a Housing Trust house. People began to appreciate the high build specifications of the trust houses and they were very sought after.

But all was not completely rosy on all Trust estates. In July 1952 the "Newsletter" carried a story about the Trust estate at Fruithill Park. It seems children had been having pitched battles with each other and also caused a great nuisance by blocking the drains with sods of earth as well as clodding them at each other and passersby.

As an estimated 8000 new homes would be needed in Belfast by

1957 the Corporation began to debate the possibility of creating a satellite town to ease the housing problem. It would take an estimated £1 million to accomplish this so no one wanted to rush into it. Providing services and refuse collection to the new estates was already causing extra expense. There was even a resistance to doing this in the Corporation and the residents of Andersonstown had to complain loud and long about the health hazard of litter and rubbish on their streets before anything was done.

Private builders were also trying to meet this housing demand but shortage of raw materials was causing them problems. Steel for

CHARLES HUTCHISON (Merok Burn Estates) LTD.
MONTGOMERY ROAD, CREGAGH ROAD, BELFAST
FOR SALE
15 Minutes from Castle Junction.
BEAUTIFUL SEMI-DETACHED RUSTIC BRICK VILLAS
Price £1,300 Net - - Deposit £130
No Legal, Road or other Charges. REPAYMENTS: 12 & 0d WEEKLY.
Apply: HEAD OFFICE, Ardmore Avenue, Finaghy. (Phone: Dunmurry 2300), or SITE OFFICE (Phone: Belfast 48000).

pipes was in short supply so many houses were fitted with aluminium pipes. Concrete slates for roofing replaced the traditional slate and breeze block faced with brick became the order of the day.

Flat concrete roofs made an appearance. Even wood was hard to get resulting in some houses being built with warped boards.

One builder cut too many corners and ran into trouble. In May 1952 the "Belfast Newsletter " reported on housing conditions in one of Belfast's fringe areas - Newtownabbey. Many young families from Belfast had moved here. Mr A. Hunter, [Unionist, Carrick] demanded an inquiry into the condition of some of the new houses. He alleged that almost all the houses were in a state of rapid deterioration. Too many corners had been cut. Soil ventilation pipes had been made to serve as part of the roof drains and there was a problem with rats.

The amazing thing is that these houses had been let and were actually occupied in spite of having no electricity installed and with gardens looking like something from the battle of Verdun.

The problem lay in the speed of construction Houses were being thrown up at a rate of five weeks from start to finish. In one area alone 226 had been erected in six months!

One hundred and three of these were subsequently found to be defective in some way. The speed of building and the fact that people were willing in spite of everything to move into these dwellings and pay rent emphasises how desperate people were to get housed.

The response of the Stormont government to Mr Hunter raising the issue is given by Capt. Terence O'Neill :

"The government has done a lot for these people and to hold it responsible for the trouble they now find themselves in was scarcely just or fair."

Presumably also categorized as "these people" would be those desperate for proper housing who turned up daily at the City Hall and patiently queued in order to enquire how far up the housing list they had progressed. Some, driven to distraction, decided to exploit any loophole in the system to get a house.

A Housing Scandal - The Copeland Case

To get a council house an applicant had to meet certain criteria which earned them points. The applicant was then placed on the waiting list. As can be seen, some people were at the end of their tether for new houses. So, there was in Belfast a deplorable level of desperation which could be exploited by the unscrupulous. The awarding of points was open to abuse.

A further layer of complication was the suspicion in the minority community that since a householder was also a rate payer with the entitlement to a vote that the Unionist dominated Belfast Corporation was preferring Protestant applicants over all others. Built in to the points system was a preference to applicants who had been members of the armed forces. People were willing to try anything to edge their application ahead of somebody else.

One way was to get your local councillor to intervene in some way on your behalf. Councillors were asked to inquire where a name was on the list or to perhaps sign a letter supporting a plea for special consideration. It was not uncommon for people to queue for hours in the rain outside a councillor's house to see if an application for a house could be advanced in any way. My own mother did it. She queued in the rain for over two hours. When she reached the front door she was told the councillor was seeing no body else that day and she was turned away. What power councillors had! They must have felt like medieval barons.

Another method was to get a doctor to support the advancement of an application by certifying that someone in the family had a serious health complaint made worse by poor housing. For example, if you could prove with a doctor's supporting letter that someone in the household had TB you would be greatly advanced on the points score.

In January 1954 the Belfast newspapers carried reports of an inquiry into allegations made against an official of the Belfast Corporation Estates Department. There were accusations of bribery and corruption in how Corporation houses were being allocated and a supervising inspector in the Corporation Estates Department, was accused of having accepted bribes to allocate houses.

By March of that year an inquiry was in full swing. The official accused was exonerated and cleared but, in the on-going inquiry twenty -three people were revealed to have paid money either directly or through a third party to a Mrs. Ann Copeland in the belief that she had a useful contact in the Estates Department who could advance their application. It seems she sent her "clients" to two doctors to seek medical certificates to include with their applications for housing.

It was outside the terms of the inquiry to decide if the doctors were guilty of professional misconduct and this matter was referred to the Medical Council. One was held by the GMC to have been involved in issuing certificates but it could not be proved he had financially benefitted from his involvement. He narrowly missed being struck off and was put on a year's probation by the Medical Council. Later, perhaps not surprisingly, Mrs Copeland was given notice to quit her Corporation house.

There was some good news by 1955 for those seeking to gain a foothold in the private housing sector.

Messrs. J and RW Taggart Ltd. advertised "A Home of your Own [with full government subsidy of £325 or £360]" was available for a deposit of £65 and an all-in weekly budget of 41/6. This was a wonderful one off offer only made possible because of a 95% Building Society advance available to owner occupiers.

What "superior modern residences "could be bought? Well, you could get a semi-detached villa in Glengormley or Cavehill for £1275-£1300 or, for a deposit of £50 and all-in weekly budget of 59/-, a detached bungalow in Jordanstown.

The All-In Weekly Budget covered:

- Repayment of the 95% Building Society loan

- Ground rent
- Rates
- Fire Insurance

Most importantly, the big selling point was that all except Jordanstown were reachable by Corporation transport. Jordanstown dwellers were simply advised to use the Ulster Transport Authority buses which served rural dwellers.

In spite of all efforts made by the Corporation, the Housing Trust and private developers the housing need had still not been met by the end of the 50s. Even a new Rent Bill had failed to help the situation It had been an attempt to force landlords to keep rented property in good repair. But the downside had been that if they did a minimum of repair it empowered them to up the rent. This meant that in poorer areas of Belfast houses which had been rented at 6/1 per week could now face an increase of 2/5 to 8/6per week making even more misery for tenants.

So, throughout the 1950s the list of applicants for new council homes grew daily and too many of Belfast's citizens continued to live in inadequate accommodation.

Work

The wealth of Belfast relied too heavily on traditional industries like ship building, linen manufacture and heavy engineering. In the aftermath of both world wars there had been slight post war booms but these proved deceptive. Like other British industrial centres Belfast by the mid 1950s faced serious challenges. Pre-war there had been little interest in improving the infrastructure in Northern Ireland and few attempts made to attract new more competitive industries. Basic raw materials like coal and steel cost much more in Northern Ireland than in other parts of the United Kingdom. Thus, in comparison with its counterparts on the mainland, Belfast was reckoned to be more disadvantaged.

Belfast was poorly placed to take on the competition in shipbuilding which would come from the recovering Germany. The Belfast Shipyard built excellent ships and the order books looked to be healthy. But the shipyard management in the '50s failed to move with the times and

TANKER LAUNCH AT QUEEN'S ISLAND—The British Skill leaving the slipways at Harland & Wolff's Musgrave Yard yesterday.

the work force stayed stuck in what were becoming outmoded practices. Ships built in Harland and Wolff's took too long to complete; too often launch dates were not met and costs became too high. Those wanting cheaper ships eventually began looking to the Far East, Germany or Scandinavia.

If the "Yard "went down so too would all its allied trades and industries.

The aircraft maker Short Brothers and Harland was just holding up by diversifying into making anything it could as well as parts for planes but like the shipyard it was heavily shored up with government money. In fact the government owned 70% of the company! It too was facing hard times ahead.

There just was not the entrepreneurial spirit which had done so much to develop nineteenth century Belfast. In a post war age of rapid technological advance Belfast seemed to have lost its fizz.

Since industry was on such a narrow base Belfast was vulnerable to every shift in world markets. Who for example in the post war austerity of the '50s needed Belfast's specialism of luxury liners? If the American market for Irish Linen sneezed, Belfast caught cold. As the bandaging on the Ulster Museum's Mummy evidences linen lasted for ever; it was not something that needed to be regularly replaced. Linen would simply not be able to compete with cheaper man -made fibres like nylon, rayon and terylene.

Unemployment remained high throughout the 1950s. The workers' experience in some trades was of cyclical employment – "lay-offs" – because there was no business on the books or, in the case of the "Yard" by finishing trades held up by shipwrights' or platers' disputes and strikes. To other workers the experience was worse. It was of permanent unemployment as firms went under or the need for particular skills could not be transferred and disappeared. Those who were unskilled labour suffered the most.

Belfast had to diversify and traditional industries adjust or Belfast would go bust!

The government at Stormont decided to act. In 1953 it passed the Aid to Industry Act which allowed the Ministry of Commerce to make subsidies to industries to help to defray the high costs of coal, gas and electricity.

It was hoped that expenditure thus saved by the industries could be directed to increasing job opportunities and modernisation. The Northern Ireland government also took it upon itself to try to upgrade the road system something which was essential with the threatened closure of the GNR rail link.

Capital grants were made to existing industries and a Northern Ireland Development Council set up to try to tackle the thorny and on-going problem of unemployment by generating new business. The government actually began to buy over old factories and to build new ones with a view to letting them By 1955 it owned 49 factories, the majority in the Belfast area. Now, new firms had to be attracted.

Step up the Belfast Corporation and the Stormont Ministry of Commerce! The Corporation campaigned vigorously for new firms to come to Belfast and the Ministry endeavoured to attract businesses by offering favourable deals on utilities and rates as well as purpose – built factory sites. The Northern Ireland government also argued time and again that the province should be treated as an area of special economic deprivation and given extra help by the central government at Westminster. The 1950s can therefore be seen as an ongoing period of adjustment and struggle to offset the demise of the traditional industries.

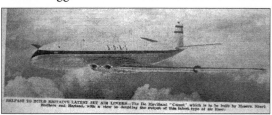

BELFAST TO BUILD BRITAIN'S LATEST JET AIR LINERS.—The De Havilland "Comet" which is to be built by Messrs. Short Brothers and Harland, with a view to doubling the output of this latest type of air liner.

CHAPTER 6

COUGHS, SNEEZES AND DISEASES

SCARLET FEVER

128 cases in Belfast

Of the 178 cases of infectious diseases notified in Belfast last week, 128 were of scarlet fever, 22 of measels, and 17 of whooping cough.

In Londonderry, there were six cases of measels and three of whooping cough.

Thirty-two cases of tuberculosis were reported by the Northern Ireland Tuberculosis Authority. Six of them were in Belfast and four in Londonderry.

THANKS TO THE INTRODUCTION of the National Health Service to Northern Ireland people who had not been able to afford to attend a doctor, dentist or optician or have hospital treatment could now do so. It is horrifying to think that the first thing some did was to have all their teeth taken out and dentures fitted!

The introduction of the new Health Service was not without hitches. The Mater Hospital had refused to come under the Northern Ireland Hospitals Authority. It maintained that it needed to maintain its voluntary status in order to protect the Roman Catholic ethos of the hospital. This meant that it would receive no state funding or grants. Funding for the hospital had to be provided by the Roman Catholic authorities and by fund-raising [among the organisations raising money was a group called "The Young Philanthropists" who ran the "YP" Pools and held concerts]. The issue of the Mater Hospital would roll on for many years after the 1950s.

Mass production of the new wonder drug Penicillin and the facility for mass immunisation programmes gradually would help to eradicate many killer diseases and an emphasis on the health and welfare of the nation would bring better times to much of the population of Belfast. No one in the '50s expected high tech' medical procedures but they did hope for basic treatment which could save discomfort and people's lives. I believe 1950s people were much more heroic about their medical problems than we are today. Take for example the reaction to the periodic outbreak of winter 'flu.

Of course nowadays, we do not just get winter 'flu we get 'flu with names. Many will recall the big scare over **Bird 'Flu** when even the family budgie came under suspicion as a possible carrier and everyone gave pigeons a wide berth. Also, how often have you heard someone say they had the 'flu when all they really had was a heavy cold?

In the first week of January 1951 a small notice appeared in all the Belfast newspapers. It read, "The wards in the City Hospital have been closed to visitors". The reason was a serious outbreak of 'flu. Symptoms included fever, diahorrea and vomiting and general pains all over the body.

Imagine a notice like that appearing today. Imagine the level of panic in the general public. The prospect of any 'flu has us scampering for germicidal hand-creams and has the Japanese travelling about in protective face masks! My impression of the reaction of the general public in the 1950s is that they took outbreaks of winter 'flu in their stride. We would be going bonkers if events today unfolded as they did in that January of 1951.

Throughout the rest of the first week of 1951 other hospitals inserted similar notices. By the end of the week 226 Post Office personnel including postmen and telephonists in Belfast and its immediate area were on sick-leave. Post-boxes had not been cleared and were full to overflowing, delivery of mail became sporadic and in some areas non-existent. Hundreds succumbed and industrial production was hit as people failed to report for work. Even the Xmas Panto' was cancelled because 24 cast members were struck down. G.Ps had to struggle through snow to do house calls.

Day on day the situation worsened with doctors and nurses going down like nine pins and the Hospitals Authority actually appealing for anyone with nursing experience to report to the nearest hospital! The most vulnerable were the very young and the old and deaths were caused not only by this 'flu but also by complications like pneumonia and bronchitis. By 9th January there were record claims for sickness benefit – 7000 – double the usual number for the time of year and the epidemic showed no sign of abating. It eventually ended after a few weeks with 61 recorded deaths from 'flu. Added to this is the fact that it was miserable in Belfast. Coal was in short supply and as a fuel economy measure, the N.I. government had followed London's example and ordered a blackout of shop windows and displays.

I think we would in this situation consider Armageddon was near. Our 1950s counterparts were made of sterner stuff. Anyway, around them there were even worse killer diseases. Four diseases had reached epidemic proportions in Belfast by 1952- Whooping Cough, Poliomyelitis, Influenza and Infectious Hepatitis!

The outbreak of Polio was frightening. Parents hurried to have their children immunised and the newspapers carried notices giving the location of the polio clinic in your neighbourhood.

Cases developing the disease were admitted to hospital and thankfully because of that quick intervention and the strain being a weak one not many sufferers developed complete paralysis.

The Infectious Hepatitis was like a bad strain of gastric 'flu and it began with children showing symptoms like appendicitis would produce. Mercifully it too was a weak strain and could be successfully treated.

Mothers dreaded the child getting the Whooping Cough. A child would cough until it vomited - there was no respite. Chemists made up their own cough bottles and much patent medicine would be spooned down the child's throat only to be sicked up again. Desperate mothers would try any old folk cure. Passing the infected child under a donkey or having the unfortunate infant wear a bag of noxious herbs made up by a "faith healer" being two tried on me. They did not work but I liked meeting the donkey. What it thought of me being pulled and hauled underneath it is not recorded.

These epidemics apart, one of the greatest killers in the early part of the twentieth century was T.B. Whole families had been wiped out by it. Signs on public transport urged passengers not to spit on the floors of buses since TB was a disease transmitted by vapour. It continued to be a killer in the 1950s but, with mass immunisation seen as the way to stop it, the 1950s also saw the gradual conquest of this disease. By 1955 there was a visible downward trend in deaths from T.B.

Treatment for T.B. was harsh with victims being isolated in T.B. or Fever hospitals such as Whiteabbey, Forster Green, or Crawfordsburn. It was believed that T.B. did not thrive in the cold so patients were subjected to a cold regime in freezing wards.

Children [if undernourished] who had been in contact with a victim were sometimes taken away and placed for a period of time in the healthier environment of a holiday home. But the best defence against the disease proved to be immunisation.

Immunisation through the BCG injection had begun in 1949 but had been restricted to certain groups such as those who had had contact with a victim and special groups like medical students, nurses, laboratory technicians, hospital staff,

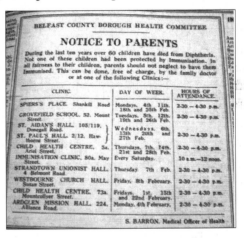

new born infants, and school leavers. Twenty-seven Chest Clinics and a mass radiography service had been set up. By 1954 there had been a vast increase in the number of those in the 10-14 years old group who had received the BCG.

This combination of effective detection of T.B. in its early stages plus immunisation to prevent it, greatly reduced the waiting lists for those waiting for treatment of the developed disease.

Another dread was Diphtheria. The '50s saw outbreaks of this horror but again by 1955 doctors were hot on its heels and the same combination of preventative measures also reduced the death rate here.

There were even reports of cases of typhoid mostly from drinking contaminated water or eating contaminated shellfish like cockles.

One good indicator of the health of a population is the rate of infant mortality. Infant mortality in Belfast had been high [in 1945 68 per 1000 live births in children under one year] so the care and health of infants and toddlers was a big concern. That is not to say that nothing had been done in this area up to the arrival of the health and welfare systems.

On 3rd January 1954 the "Newsletter" carried an obituary of Mrs. Hannah Mary Baker – the founder of The Belfast Babies' Clubs. She was an Englishwoman who had come over with her husband to live in Belfast before World War 1. Belfast owes Mrs. Baker and her helpers a lot.

Mrs. Baker realised that young mothers who were poor and with sick babies had nowhere to go for advice and support. Together with two woman doctors she set up a support group – the Babies' Club. Mothers brought their children once a week to be weighed and free advice was given on health and nutrition. Baby clothes which had been knitted by volunteers were given free. Even when the Health Service took over the clinics those using them still called them Babies' Clubs and the newspapers of the '50s carry photos of large happy groups of mothers and children often going off on organised outings to the seaside. By 1955 the rate of infant mortality per 1000 live births had decreased to 32.4. This was still high since in England and Wales at the same time it was 25. I love the idea that the clubs were non-sectarian because the members were the babies who had no notion of such things.

Living through childhood itself was a risky business. Children fell prey to a wide variety of ailments- measles, mumps, chicken-pox, scarlet fever. These are not so prevalent today again thanks to immunisation programmes. In the '50s they were really feared. They could be life limiting as they had the potential to cause deafness, blindness, brain damage and scarring. In the worst cases children died.

The preventative measure against any child hood illness was to "build the child up". Children had free milk in school, free orange juice and big spoonfuls of Cod Liver Oil. Virol [a sweet sticky gooey mixture which was supposed to be full of vitamins] Castor Oil and Syrup of Figs were regularly ladled into them. Any youngster found scratching its backside was given a Worm Ball! Any outbreaks and those not already immunised would be taken to the doctor to be perforated with an injection needle the width of a tree trunk.

The most important reason for keeping children healthy was to get them to school. Buttoned into rubber- buttoned Liberty Bodices and vests, with woollen scarves wrapped across their chests and fastened with a big safety pin at the back, heads enclosed in snoods or balaclava helmets and crammed full of cough syrup the youngster with a cold was packed off to school. Staying off was not an option. In the days before paper hankies with balm to protect little noses children would be packed off to obliterate sneezes and snot in one of their father's big white hankies.

Mothers on whom all the worry had taken its toll were urged to fortify themselves with "Wincarnis" or "Buckfast" tonic wines to restore their nerves. If overconsumption threatened to damage the liver they could always turn to "Bile Beans" guaranteed to "Wake Up Your Liver Bile".

Getting your child through childhood, getting it educated, finding a good house and keeping a job may have pre-occupied most of people's time but there were other worries too about the Cold War and the H-bomb. However, there were things to distract from all these woes.

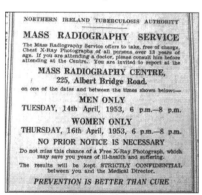

NORTHERN IRELAND TUBERCULOSIS AUTHORITY

MASS RADIOGRAPHY SERVICE

The Mass Radiography Service offers to take, free of charge, Chest X-Ray Photographs of all persons over 13 years of age. If you are attending a doctor, please consult him before attending at the Centre. You are invited to report at the

MASS RADIOGRAPHY CENTRE,
225, Albert Bridge Road.

on one of the dates and between the times shown below:—

MEN ONLY
TUESDAY, 14th April, 1953, 6 p.m.—8 p.m.

WOMEN ONLY
THURSDAY, 16th April, 1953, 6 p.m.—8 p.m.

NO PRIOR NOTICE IS NECESSARY

Do not miss this chance of a Free X-Ray Photograph, which may save you years of ill-health and suffering.

The results will be kept STRICTLY CONFIDENTIAL between you and the Medical Director.

PREVENTION IS BETTER THAN CURE

The new Maternity Unit, which was formerly the hospital for infectious diseases.

New maternity unit at City Hospital

"Gardner Robb House" opened by Judge Robb

MORE "POLIO" IN BRITAI

Schools still close area

As hundreds of childr to some Burton-on-Tr schools which were yesterday after a week in infantile paralysis

CHAPTER 7

RADIO AND TELEVISION

I N THE '40s AND early '50s Belfast people in common with those throughout Northern Ireland were loyal radio listeners. Most houses in Belfast had a radio. The 1950s radio was a large weighty object requiring a well put up shelf or substantial piece of furniture to hold it. Valve operated, it had to "warm up" before it would transmit and the valves emitted a mysterious glow. The high quality radio could access Medium Wave, Long Wave and even Short Wave. Twiddling the tuning dial was like taking a short tour of the North and East of Europe from far flung Bratislava, Hilversum, Riga, Radio Moscow, Vilnius, Vatican Radio, Berlin to the closer to home Athlone and Droitwich.

At the end of the war the BBC took stock of the programmes which were on offer to the listening public. In war time it had been important to keep up the morale of the nation especially in factories. Programmes like "Workers' Playtime", comedy programmes like "I.T.M.A." and the "General Forces Programme " had been popular with audiences. So, post war, a continuation of these forms of entertainment seemed the way to go. The Light Programme was born. It provided popular radio entertainment with music, variety shows and serials. This was joined in the scheduling by the already existing Home Service which was the main channel for the news and more serious programmes and the Third Programme [the Third Programme broadcast concerts of classical music together with serious talks and discussions catering for small esoteric audiences who have always down to the present proved fiercely loyal to it].

The Light Programme had all sorts of shows by the big comedians of the day such as Charlie Chester, Arthur Askey and Tommy Trinder. Popular shows included "Meet the Huggetts", "Hancock's Half Hour", "Much Binding in the Marsh", and "Life with the Lyons". It had music from Billy Cotton and the first of the soaps, "The Archers" and "Mrs. Dale's Diary". "The Archers" (simple farming folk) occupied fictional Ambridge and the character Doris Archer actually died on air in 1955. Mrs. Dale was the fictional wife of a doctor about whom she appeared to be perpetually worried. In the clipped middle class accent of the time the actress playing her, Jesssie Mathews would lament, "Em terribly worried about Jem." She had a rather grand sister called "Selly" and a cat called "Keptin". The Belfast housewife going about her morning chores only needed to stay within earshot of the radio to keep up with all Mrs. Dale's latest traumas.

On Sundays there was "Family Favourites" or "The Navy Lark". You could even waltz and quickstep around your own living room to Victor Sylvester and his dance band. One puzzling show was "Educating Archie" which was fronted by a ventriloquist and his dummy, the aforementioned "Archie". Could radio listeners tell whether the ventriloquist's lips moved or not?

The only station to give The Light Programme a run for its money was Radio Luxembourg with its quiz shows. Calling itself "The Station Of The Stars" it featured daily sponsored record programmes during the 1950's

Children had very few radio programmes dedicated to them until the coming of schools' radio broadcasts perhaps that is why children's television when it came proved so popular with them. There were 'Listen with Mother', a short 15 minute slot at about 1.45pm every day for the tots and on Saturday mornings Uncle Mac and "Children's

Favourites". Uncle Mac began with, "Hello children everywhere!" and would play music which children requested and could enthusiastically sing along to.

Among the favourites were:

"Giily Gilly Osenfeffer Katzenellen Bogen by the sea" [Max Bygraves]

"The Ugly Duckling" [Danny Kaye]

"The Runaway Train" [Michael Holiday]

"Nellie the Elephant" [Mandy Miller]

"How much is that Doggy in the Window?"[Lita Rosa] and

"Bimbo" [Suzi Miller].

Northern Ireland people actually preferred the Northern Ireland Home Service to the nationally broadcast Light Programme. They were then as now avid listeners to "The News". Also much loved was Joseph Tumelty's "The McCooeys a serial about an ordinary Belfast family of "unidentifiable religious background" ["The Most Contrary Region. The B.B.C. in Northern Ireland 1924-1984. Rex Cathcart] It ran for seven years from 1949 until 1956 when Tumelty because of a serious accident had to stop writing.

"The McCooeys" attracted a listening public of half a million listeners to its Saturday evening and Monday repeat. It was even loved outside the province as it could be picked up by listeners in Ayrshire and the west coast of Scotland. The cast featured a host of Ulster actors including J.G. Devlin, Stephen Boyd, James Young, Audrey Bell, Sheila McGibbon, John McBride and of course the author himself Joseph Tumelty.

"What is the secret of its success?" asked Henry McMullen in the "B.B.C. Yearbook for 1951"-

"Probably the answer is their normality.............There is a warmth and humanity in "The McCooeys" home which has reached the listener and brought him back week after week to his loudspeaker."

After "The McCooeys went off air in 1957 B.B.C. N. I. tried hard to find a replacement. At first they tried to copy the "Mrs. Dale's Diary" formula with "The Carlisles" but it never succeeded in capturing the audience. Then the playwright Jack Loudan had a go with the more successful "Mrs. Lally's Lodgers".

But for Northern Ireland listeners nothing was quite the same as the legendary magic of Tumelty's, "The McCooeys".

On another front a radio breakthrough of a different kind was taking place in Northern Ireland. The historians T.W. Moody and J. C.Beckett worked with other historians who were keen to revise the 1950s view of important events in Irish History and produced a series of programmes called, "Ulster Since 1800". This groundbreaking series challenged accept views of the past and tried to create a public history which was both accessible and objective. It represented a major and highly influential shift in the interpretation of Irish history

By 1953 close to five hundred schools in Northern Ireland had stated they wished to receive schools programmes. The BBC NI did not feel it necessary to create special programmes for Northern Ireland schools so it simply imported existing ones. School radios were big wooden boxes which were carried into a classroom at the appropriate time in the week and plugged into the aerial in the wall then, off things went.

Firm favourite with the schools was, "Music and Movement" where children were told to listen to a piece of piano music and then imagine themselves to be the wind or a tree – this could be a big stretch for some! Crawling on all fours around a classroom full of pupils and wooden desks or, rushing about as the wind, would nowadays be considered a health and safety nightmare. Not so in the 1950s classroom. There was also the serialised story- "Jennings" or "Just William" – children had mighty powers of listening and concentration in those days.

Then there was "Singing Together". Every child would be issued with a song book and from the big radio box at the front of the room would come the piano accompaniment. Thus Belfast children would stand at their desks and merrily gulder away to what were essentially British folk songs like, "Where have you been all the day Billy Boy?" to which the reply was that Billy Boy had been with his Nancy who "tickled his fancy". Try getting a modern P4 through that! Any survivor of "Singing Together "can quite happily warble their way through "Men of Harlech", "Westering Home" or "It is the month of Maying" but may draw a blank at anything remotely Irish. The nearest my own P5 class got to an Irish folk number was "The Minstrel Boy" and that caused a local incident. A warm day, all the classroom windows were wide to the street outside. We were at full belt when the door went to the wall with a thud. In strode a local mother and well known two flags out the bedroom window loyalist. "Here you," she shouted at the teacher, "Stop that Fenian nonsense!"

To her credit the teacher, a "bunty" wee woman who took no prisoners, frog marched her out of the school. Then followed an altercation in the playground. The radio took no account of this drama and since this was a new song to be learnt told us to sing it again. By the time the teacher returned we were on a very sotto voce second verse.

The post war flowering of radio was soon to be challenged by the arrival of T.V. Mr. Kelso had demonstrated in January 1950 the inability of getting T.V. pictures from the transmitter in Sutton Coalfield in the English Midlands but what if a transmitter was to be established here in Belfast? A quick glance at the table setting out the number of receiving licences will clearly indicate the impact of the erection on the hills above the city of that longed for B.B.C T.V. transmitting aerial

Wireless Receiving Licences [Sound and Vision] in each year ending 31st March.

	Sound	Television
1950	200,750	-
1951	205,975	2
1952	212,250	55
1953*	215,187	558
1954	222,989	10,353
1955	218,967	23,808
1956	205,451	42,206
1957	193,218	63,348
1958	178,655	85,490
1959**	161,892	106,588

*Coronation Year ** Arrival of U.T.V.

The Arrival of Television

"Television is a national monopoly and Northern Ireland as a loyal part of the United Kingdom should not be excluded from this development", so announced the Radio Retailers Association of Northern Ireland in March 1952. One suspects that what was energising the minds of the retailers was the rumour of a possibility that the forthcoming Coronation might be broadcast on T.V. The radio retailers were experiencing a slump because in anticipation people had cancelled orders for new radios and were hoping to buy T.Vs instead. The new Pye factory in Larne actually tried to put a bit of pressure on the Stormont government to use a bit of political clout by threatening that they needed T.V. broadcasting in Northern Ireland for the factory to stay in production.

In October 1952 hopes of anyone in Great Britain viewing the Coronation via T.V. seemed to be dashed when the Earl Marshall, the Duke of Norfolk, announced it would not be broadcast. The Pathe News was to be allowed to film the ceremony and show it in full colour in cinemas instead. However very soon after this hopes were raised again that at least some part of the occasion would be shown on the T.V.

The pressure was on to get a T.V. transmitter for Northern Ireland and so the BBC in January 1953 announced that there would be a temporary station at Glencairn. This meant that viewing would be confined to the proximity of Belfast itself. This was enough to set the number of orders for TVs soaring and dealers predicted a demand for 10,000 sets in Northern Ireland alone. The electronics manufacturer Cossor confidently anticipated a demand throughout Britain for over a million sets and actually held a demonstration of their latest models in Belfast. Interest in TVs may be gauged by the fact that over 2000 radio dealers from across the province turned up to view the sets.

The new TVs were an imposing piece of furniture. The polished mahogany or teak casing housed a modest 12 inch or 14 inch screen but took up a whole corner of the room. In the 1950s they were to become a status symbol. As can be seen from the adverts for T.V. sets they were not cheap but everything was placed within reach of a purchaser by virtue of Hire Purchase. H.P. really had taken off. People moving from small houses to larger ones did not have enough furniture or wanted to replace the plain Utility furniture manufactured in war time.

What could be better than the "never- never" of Hire Purchase. So many people began to use it that concern was expressed in the Senate at Stormont and a demand for some regulation of its use ensued.

As the date for the Coronation, approached sales of TVs soared. The ceremony for the first time in history was to be viewed not just by the privileged aristocracy but by T.V. viewers nationwide. The argument about broadcasting the event switched now to one of how to ensure that the viewers could be guaranteed to be conducting themselves with the correct reverence and awe. The Archbishop of Canterbury, Dr. Fisher, appealed for a sort of mass participation from all those viewing in their homes or on the public screens throughout the country. They were urged to join in the singing of the hymns and to be reverent during the prayers. It was hoped men would remove their hats once the Westminster Abbey broadcast began.

His plea would not fall on deaf ears given the mood of '50s Ulster when many people were known to stand up in the privacy of their own homes every time the National Anthem was played on the radio!

On the day itself Belfast was bathed in glorious sunshine whereas London experienced torrential downpours. Hundreds of people queued from 7a.m. at Bellevue as the Floral Hall had a public T.V. showing. Families brought picnics and made the best of the day. People with TVs likely as not had packed houses full of family, friends and neighbours eagerly awaiting the broadcast to kick off at 10.15. Many churches had opened their church halls for people to come together to listen to the radio transmission.

For television broadcasting this was a groundbreaking day both nationally and in the province. The procession to Westminster Abbey, the whole ceremony, a balcony appearance by the Royal family were all seen and the day's broadcasting closed with coverage of the fireworks display – all of course in glorious black and white.

Outside of Belfast people had had to rely on the radio to experience the day and waited for the Pathe News film. Interestingly enough this had been banned from being shown in the Republic of Ireland. So hundreds of people came north to see it in cinemas in Northern Ireland. In some border areas cinema managers actually estimated that 60% of the audience for the film was from the South and at least one train packed full of people eager to see the film had run from south to north

By 1954 there were plans in the pipeline for more transmitters to be erected across the province to bring T.V. broadcasts to a wider audience and in July the Divis transmitter opened. This extended T.V. to eighty percent of the population as far as Ardglass and Newry in the South, Coleraine in the north and Dungannon in the West. So powerful was the new transmitter that those living close to it in the Belfast area had to have their sets adjusted because of the distortion on their screens. Everyone who owned a 1950s, '60s T.V. will remember the small series of knobs on the front or back to adjust horizontal and vertical hold and the frequency with which the picture could whirl up and down as if someone was turning a handle on the side of a set.

In Larne problems with interference came from another source. Viewers were thwarted because their T.V. picture was ruined by interference from a masseur's machine which was on the same frequency as the Divis transmitter. The owner of the offending apparatus was reluctant to change the frequency as he was afraid that to do so would "retard" his machine.

The Post Office now issued licences for TV and detector vans went around Belfast looking for T.V. aerials and checking ownership. This in turn revealed the existence of "TV snobs"- sort of wanna-be social

climbers. These were people who could not afford TVs but wanted to give the impression that they owned one. So, they had a TV aerial erected on the roof of their house. "Keeping up with the Joneses" gone mad.

Other Belfast people who could not afford TV sets resorted to ingenious methods of seeing their favourite programmes. Friends or relatives with sets regularly found themselves inundated with "guests". Shops selling TVs turned them on at night in a window display and there is a report of one family complete with deck chairs and a bag of sweets each settled down outside a retailer's for a night's viewing.

By 1955 bigger and better sets were on display at the Earl's Court Radio Show. The 12 and 14 inch screens were to be replaced by 17 and even 21 inch ones. There was even for a dizzy £525 the ultimate piece of kit - a super T.V. housing a 21 ins screen, radio, record player, tape recorder and........refrigerated bar!

What was a typical day's viewing like for Belfast viewers at the beginning of the '50s? BBC Northern Ireland at first produced few programmes of regional interest so local audiences were treated to what was available nationally. The viewing public was not the wide cross section of people the radio had to cater for. Radio coped by having a clear differentiation in its programming. It created different programmes for the different audiences to its Light, Home and Third programmes. BBC television had no option but a "one size fits all" approach.

This produced a very mixed bag of programmes with those of an improving or documentary nature predominating. A glance at the programming for 21st August 1954 demonstrates this point.

At 3.30 – 4 pm TV tried to woo the "Mrs. Dale's Diary" audience away from the radio with an attempt at what they hoped would be a popular programme, "Fabian of the Yard" but then probably drove them back to the Light Programme with a mind - numbing documentary, "Wealth from the Wilderness" followed up with a play, "The Apollo of Bellac" by Giraudoux. One wonders what they thought the demographic of the viewing audience was.

A break in transmission was not an unusual occurrence. Breaks would be covered by "The Interlude" when music would be played and a picture shown of horses ploughing a field or someone working a potter's wheel. A kitten playing with a ball of wool was very popular.

BILLY BUNTER ENTERS TELEVISION—An episode at Greyfriars School came to life yesterday in the children's television programme. The series, consisting of separate events from the famous school stories, will feature Gerald Campion as Billy Bunter, the fat boy.

Children were catered for with programmes like the cartoon adventures of the boxer pup, "Bengo", and other curious cartoon offerings like "Noggin the Nog". Puppets predominated. The producers counted on the naivety or very poor eyesight of the juvenile audience; four strings could clearly be seen on "Andy Pandy" and" Muffin the Mule". Children also loved the pure anarchy of "Sooty"; the little glove puppet was a constant torture to his human operator Harry Corbett.

Then there were the precursors of the "Teletubbies", the "gubalupping" "Bill and Ben the Flowerpot Men". In this programme "Little Weed" and the narrator were the only ones to speak comprehensible English and all she ever said was, "Oh, Weed, Little Weed".

For older children there was "Crackerjack" hosted by a curiously wooden and slightly embarrassed ex-boxing commentator, Eamonn Andrews. Each time he mentioned the name of the show the audience bellowed back, "Crackerjack". The whole show had the air of a mini pantomime about it. Among the other delights was the less salubrious goings-on at Grayfriars School of "the owl of the Remove", Billy Bunter. Bunter was supposed to be a fat, obnoxious boy in about Fourth Form – strangely he was played by a man in his thirties! The annoying hapless "Mr Pastry" brought a perhaps ancient ancestor of Mr.Bean to the screen and the story-teller Shirley Abacair with her zither sang everybody into a completely comatose state.

Children liked American imports such as the adventures of "Champion the Wonder Horse" - a wonderful creature who righted wrongs in the old West. A quick burst of the "William Tell Overture" which was the theme music for another import, "The Lone Ranger", will bring back memories to many of the masked avenger, his faithful side kick, Tonto and the Ranger's cry to his big white horse of, "Hi Ho Silver – Away!" There was nothing politically correct about this programme. The all-American Lone Ranger was the brains of the outfit and Tonto was an uneducated "Injun" who could barely speak English except to address the Ranger reverentially as "Kemosabee". However, Tonto was ace at listening for hoof beats and following trails.

The Ranger actually visited Belfast in August 1958 as a promotion for his full length feature film, "The Lone Ranger and the City of Gold". He made a live appearance at the Grand Opera House which was showing the film and then startled the waitresses at the Grand Central Hotel when he made an appearance at breakfast the next morning in full costume plus mask. Tonto and Silver gave Belfast a miss.

The BBC also wanted children's T.V. viewing to be culturally  improving and so the classic serial was born. Reams of Dickens serialised and broadcast on Sunday evenings around 5.30pm. became compulsory family viewing in many homes.

The BBC did try Variety with some American imports such as Christmas Specials like "The Perry Como Show". Billy Cotton was persuaded from radio to a Saturday night T.V. show and the popular magician David Nixon had his own show- the medium of television being ideal for his kind of close magic. There was "Six Five Special" to cater for the pop mad teenager and the T.V. soap was born with "The Groves" and "Dixon of Dock Green". There were documentaries.

One curious one was made by SCUBA experts Hans and Lotte Hasse. With somewhat stilted commentary and murky photography these two intrepids aimed to reveal to the viewing public the wonders of the deep. "Look now how Hans is being chased by ze conger eel".

Northern Ireland's first live T.V. broadcast was "Press Conference" broadcast in November 1955. In it the Prime Minister of Northern Ireland, Lord Brookborough spoke nationwide from his room in Stormont. Making an obviously snide attack on the Republic of Ireland he assured mainland viewers that Ulstermen were not stage Irishmen.

They did not carry shillelaghs, wear swallow-tail coats or battered bowler hats but were people loyal to the Crown. Ulster people he said were a resilient and hard working "individualistic race". He also referred to the then current IRA border campaign as "stupid".

Going on to disparage nationalist M.P.s at Stormont Brookborough said," If you started a discussion on eggs they would say we were treating nationalist hens the wrong way."

Quite obviously he saw the broadcast as a golden opportunity to extol the glories as he saw it of Northern Ireland. But he and other unionists were to prove a bit hyper-sensitive when it came to what others broadcast about Northern Ireland.

In January 1959 the BBC was forced to make an apology over an episode of the "Tonight" programme. Unionist feathers had been severely ruffled by how Belfast had been portrayed in this programme. Unionists complained that the reporting team from the mainland had gone out of its way to film the seedy side of the city – back alleys, betting shops and queues at the "Broo". The whole impression created was thus of a dingy, dirty city. A letter to the "Belfast Newsletter" from a Lisburn correspondent is revealing about the unionist mindset. The writer makes no secret of his political and religious affiliation when he states,"...in regard to the part of the film showing people going to Church, well, in all my life I've never seen such a motley crowd.....it is very evident these people were not going to a Protestant church."

Further outrage was caused in April of that year by the BBC broadcasting an episode of a CBS produced programme, "Small World". The participants were Ed Murrow, Noel Coward, James Thurber and Belfast born actress Siobhan McKenna; the topic under discussion was humour. Somehow or other McKenna managed to ignore the topic and when given an opening by Murrow launched into a vitriolic attack on the British P.M. Harold MacMillan for his protest at de Valera's recent release of IRA internees. She then compounded the situation by describing the IRA then engaged in a violent border campaign in Northern Ireland as "idealistic young men".

Unionists understandably went ballistic! An official protest was sent to the Director-General of the BBC by the government of Northern Ireland on behalf of the people of Northern Ireland thus ignoring the fact that some may have been in agreement with the actress Stormont Minister Brian Faulkner and the Westminster MP for West Belfast, Patricia McLaughlin both resigned from the BBC Advisory Council and Ulster MPs raised the matter in the House of Commons. Lord Brookborough in a statement actually said Siobhan McKenna should be put across somebody's knee and spanked

By August 1959 adverts began to appear in the newspapers trumpeting the opening of Ulster Television broadcasts on 31st October. Viewers were promised all kinds of treats on Channel 9 – "Emergency Ward 10", "Double Your Money", "Sunday Night at the London Palladium"- being just a few. There were also a host of American imports such as "Wagon Train", "Maverick" and "The Invisible Man". Young and old alike eagerly anticipated watching, "Robin Hood" and "Ivanhoe". [People in a particular age group can actually still sing the theme songs] How would the BBC compete with this plethora of half hour blockbusters on offer from UTV?

At first the BBC tried to gain an upper hand by suggesting that the television adverts which funded UTV would seriously disrupt the enjoyment of viewing. But UTV hit back assuring the public that Hamlet would not disrupt a soliloquy to advertise which toothpaste was preferred at Elsinore. In fact viewers liked the novelty of the ads. Advertising slogans like "Go well, Go Shell" and "I told them Oldham" featured in everyday speech and everyone wanted "the Colgate ring of confidence".

UTV made a point of emphasising how regional it was by purposefully recruiting local talent to front the station. Jimmy Greene, a local actor, Brian Durkin [local amateur actor and teacher], Ivor Mills, another local teacher became continuity announcers. They were joined in front of the camera by twenty-one year old Belfast actress Adrienne McGuill and a nineteen year old Civil Servant Anne Gregg. Local sportsman Ernest Strathdee became the Sportscaster.

As the 31st October drew near there was a complete sell out of the "TV Post" as viewers planned their viewing between the two TV channels now being offered. 100,000 across the province would be tuning in.

At 4,15pm on the 31st Channel 9 [UTV] opened with great solemnity and a pretence of high culture. The Governor of Northern Ireland, Lord Wakehurst, performed· the opening ceremony. The first person seen performing was Sir Lawrence Olivier who read with due Shakespearean delivery a long poem. Then came a locally produced programme, "Tales of Ulster" fronted by local historian and story-teller Richard Hayward. To those wanting "Robin Hood" this was all yawningly boring. But then once the preliminaries were out of the way eager viewers were treated to a sampler of the programmes they could expect from Channel 9. A typical evening's viewing would be full of treats with not much time being given over to news and documentaries. "Robin Hood and his Merry Men" at 6.30pm was followed by a cavalcade of half hour shows starting with "I Love Lucy", "Double Your Money", "Dial 999", "Wagon Train" and there was nearly always a feature film.

The BBC countered this with an evening's viewing of "This is your Life", "Panorama", International Figure Skating and "Come Dancing". Which channel would you have tuned to?

However, by 1959, the BBC was at least winning in the big Christmas head-to-head. On Christmas day it had films, Chipperfield's Circus, "The Billy Cotton Band Christmas Party", "Christmas Night With The Stars" plus a specially adapted for television version of Dickens' "Bleak House". In contrast UTV made little concession to Christmas and stuck with its usual schedule of shows.

With the arrival of T.V. came the T.V. critic. The "Newsletter" critic was J.F.C.- an individual who did not mince his or her words. In a memorable critique of a week's programmes in December 1955 JFC lambasted the offerings of the previous week –"describing them as "cretinous". The" Dave King Show" came in for most vitriol

"....the most rewarding part of "The Dave King Show" was a blessed interval when a breakdown in sound transmission afforded an all too short surcease from the waves of din that were pouring out of my set."

Another variety programme "Show Band" fared no better-"the most pleasing item was an announcement that it was the last of the series".

J.F.C. was also appalled by the appearance on one of these shows of Eamonn Andrews. "I was somewhat dismayed at the appearance of that accomplished broadcaster......Got up in an absurd Wild West outfit he gave us a very hammy and mawkish recitation. It recalled that social menace of the old-time village concert, the local bore, whom nothing could deter from inflicting on his patient audience "The Shooting of Dan Magrew" followed –applause or not- by "The Green Eye of the Little Yellow God".

They don't write them like that anymore!

By the end of the '50s with two TV channels to choose from radio, though listened to during the day, began to be replaced by TV in the evenings and its great era was ending.

In December 1959 a listener to the radio show, "Housewives Choice" requested a song to remind her of her lovely holiday in Northern Ireland. The show played, "South of the Border". That sort of thing just did not help!

NEW BELFAST CHURCH—The Church of the Epiphany, Skilly Park, Finaghy, which will be formally opened on Saturday.

CHAPTER 8

BUT – IS IT ART?

1950S BELFAST WAS NO cultural wasteland. Art lovers, music lovers, theatre goers could all find plenty of exhibitions, concerts, opera performances and plays to satisfy them. Indeed they were at times spoilt for choice. Concerts were put on by the Belfast Philharmonic Society which gave a subscription series every year, other concerts were given by the City of Belfast Orchestra and there were those sponsored by C.E.M.A.[the Council for the Encouragement of Music and the Arts which was the forerunner of the Arts Council of Northern Ireland] and The Young Philanthropists. World renowned performers and conductors appeared in Belfast regularly.

Opera lovers had two weeks of delights when the Carl Rosa Company paid its annual visit to the Opera House. In March 1956 in the first week of its tour the Company performed "Cavallaria Rusticana" and "I Paliacci", "Rigoletto", "Manon Lescaut", "The Barber of Seville", "La Boheme" and "Il Trovatore". In week two they gave "Faust", a repeat performance of "The Barber of Seville", a matinee of "Cavallaria Rusticana" and " I Paliacci" and evening performances of "Don Giovanni", "La Boheme", "Tannhauser" and "Rigoletto". Truly an amazing array of popular opera favourites.

But, what was the standard of performance like? The "Newsletter" revue of "Cavallaria Rusticana" gives some idea. The reviewer was not that impressed. The opera was sung in English. The principal soprano was judged "o.k. in the voice department" but lacking "in the variety of her arm movement" and the lead tenor appears to have given up on any attempt at acting and just stood stock still centre stage and sung.

No one appears to have held back on their criticism if they felt an attempt at culture failed to meet the mark. In January 1955 an exhibition of Italian Art 1910-1920 at the Art Gallery, Stranmillis Road caused Councillor Irene McAlery, a member of the Belfast Corporation Arts Committee, to take up cudgels. Councillor McAlery was acidic in her assessment of the worth of the art displayed:

"...if children from a nursery school had turned out some of them one would have admired their industry but would not have called it art."

The Art critic of the "Newsletter" was prompted to mount a defence in which he took a mighty and somewhat snooty swipe at non-devotees of modern art like Councillor McAlery who were written off as uncultured low-brows with a "limited understanding of assessment and a confused idea of the meaning of beauty".

A few days later Councillor McAlery was speaking at "Any Questions" in Windsor Women's Unionist Association. The question, "A waste of paint and time?" was put to her and the point made that some of the paintings had been valued at £40,000. An undeterred Miss McAlery pulled no punches when she said she would not give £25 for the lot frames and all!

The general public's reaction to the exhibition is worth noting. People flocked to see the paintings and on January 26th a school party of fifty had made the journey from Magherafelt to Belfast to attend.

In 1958 the Ulster Academy's Art Exhibition at the Stranmillis Gallery was opened by its President, William Conor. The quality of art on display must have been tremendous. The Ulster Academy had dropped its usual format of showing over 400 piece of work and at this exhibition chose to hang only forty selected paintings. Displaying their work were the then up and coming artists, Basil Blackshaw, Tom Carr and T.P. Flanagan. Conor exhibited for the first time his piece, "Shipyard Worker".

Attempts to bring culture to the young sometimes ended in disaster. A group of R.A.D.A students attempted to give a performance of "Macbeth" to a Belfast audience of school children in April 1959. It ended badly. The children were not impressed with either Shakespeare or the production. Everytime the three witches appeared they were greeted with shouts of," Here come the Beverley Sisters!". The unappreciative audience then proceeded to bombard the actors with Imperial Mints. The dialogue was drowned out by the children's talk and some booing. Either the RADA students had just met a very discerning juvenile audience or Saturday morning Children's Cinema Clubs had a lot to answer for.

Adult theatre goers in Belfast were confronted with a wide choice. Besides touring companies at the Grand Opera House and occasionally at The Empire plus a host of amateur productions, Belfast had three theatres the Lyric, the Arts and the Group. Each had its own company and performed a contrasting repertoire of plays.

The Lyric Theatre began as a private venue at the back of the home of Pearse and Mary O'Malley. The tiny theatre was created at first in Ulsterville Avenue and then when the O'Malleys moved to Derryvolgie Avenue over the former stables there. The Lyric's small enthusiastic group of actors established a formidable reputation by staging Irish plays with a Yeats' poetic drama as an annual anchor production. The Lyric also gave performances of plays from all over the world and sponsored poetry readings, art exhibitions and drama workshops. In February 1957 a literary magazine,"Threshold", edited by Mary O'Malley and having no less a person than John Hewitt as the poetry editor was published. At the proposed cost of £25,000 the Lyric eventually announced in 1959 that it would build its own new theatre at Stranmillis.

The Arts Theatre also began as a small venture which grew under the direction of its actor/manager, Hubert Wilmont. With the support of his wife, Dorothy, Hubert Wilmot set up a small theatre in an attic in Upper North Street. As the Arts grew in popularity it moved in 1954 to a disused auction room in Little Donegal Street and then finally settled in a new purpose built theatre in Botanic Avenue in 1961. Both it and the Lyric attracted a largely middle class audience for their straight dramas. In the Arts plays by Ionesco, Bolt, Arthur Millar and Cocteau were staged. A big feather in the cap of the Arts was the first production outside of America of Koestler's, "Darkness at Noon" in August 1952.

People who would not venture to the scholarly "Lyric" productions flocked to see their lives portrayed on stage by the Group Theatre Company. Many well known Ulster actors who made it big in theatre

74

and film found a start in the Ulster Group Theatre. These included Colin Bleakley, James Ellis, J.G. Devlin. Joseph Tumelty, Harold Golblatt, Stephen Boyd and Harry Towb to name but a few. The Group company staged plays with a local background and encouraged local writers to contribute.

The most notable contributor was Joseph Tumelty. His plays such as "All Souls' Night" and "Is the Priest at Home?" became very popular with the local audience. Audiences also loved St. John Ervine's "Boyd's Shop". In these plays the Group tended to diffuse controversy with a touch of humour.

"BOYD'S SHOP" ON TELEVISION—A scene from Mr. St. John Ervine's play, which was repeated on the B.B.C. Television Service last night. From left: Agnes Boyd (Sheila Monahan), the Rev. Ernest Dunwoody (Robin Bailey), Miss M'Clurg (Maureen Pryor), and Andrew Boyd (Joseph Tumelty).

But the Group could be less cosy and a play produced in 1958 on the difficult theme of sectarianism in Belfast created trouble for the company. The play so frightened the local Council for the Encouragement of Music and the Arts [C.E.M.A.] that it threatened to exercise censorship by withdrawing funding. The play in question, directed by Tyrone Guthrie, was Gerard McLarnon's, "The Bonefire".

Originally the company staged the play in the Grand Opera House, Belfast. The action was placed on an Eleventh of July Night and the events surrounding a Roman Catholic family living in a Protestant district. Star -crossed young lovers in the form of a Protestant girl and a Roman Catholic sailor also featured in a sub-plot. They ended up in a suicide pact! According to the reviews given by theatre critics the audience was nearly driven mad by the confusion of the structure of the play and the wild sound effects of loud music from Orange bands and the shouting of crowds around the off stage bonfire.

The play was badly written but it still managed to play to packed houses. The people of Belfast thus proved less sensitive than the unionist politicians who were outraged that any play attracting government and city council funding should dare to portray Belfast in a poor light.

"Roamer" the theatre critic of the "Newsletter" wrote of the production on 8th September 1958:

".....it represents a Roman Catholic view of the Protestant versus Catholic rivalry in the humbler streets of Belfast....To be fair, to have been a real plea for tolerance, the play ought to have said there is the Protestant pot and the Roman Catholic kettle, one as black as the other.....The Orange Order identified with the mob has now had..... one of its worst advertisements."

Worse was to follow when the Group was invited to transfer their production to the prestigious Edinburgh Festival. Unionists wanted the play stopped. Pressure was brought to bear on C.E.M.A. which cleverly said it only had a remit for financing plays staged in the province and so could provide no money for the Edinburgh production. Belfast City council's Lord Mayor, Cecil McKee, also played a cunning hand. Realizing the council could be accused of political censorship if it withdrew funding he called for alterations to be made to the play "in the interest of even handedness".

Though the author fulminated against changing a word amendments were made to the play. It was claimed these were only for clarity of staging! The play then went to Edinburgh and from there to the dust bin of history. No one today really recalls the controversy it caused but its claim to fame must be that it paved the way for what surely has to be one of the greatest Ulster and Irish plays of the twentieth century Sam Thompson's expose of hatred and sectarianism, "Over the Bridge".

Sam Thompson a former shipyard worker approached the young actor/director James Ellis with his play in 1959. It was to be a Group Theatre production. Thompson in his writing for radio and stage clearly displays the belief that the working class both Protestant and Catholic had been manipulated into sectarianism and purposefully prevented from making common cause on social and economic issues. In "Over the Bridge" he confronts his audience in a brutal way.

The background of the play is the Belfast shipyard. The bridge referred to in the title is the one which workers cross from Protestant Ballymacarret into the "Yard". The action of the play is about a Protestant trade union official who chooses to stand by a Roman Catholic workmate who has been threatened. The culmination of the play is the frenzied attack on both men by a sectarian mob of fellow workers which leaves the Protestant dead and the Catholic mangled.

The very prospect of this play being put on alarmed the authorities. The Belfast shipyard was at the time competing for orders and in a shaky state – what effect would this play have on that? "The Bonefire " had been challenging; "Over the Bridge" could be catastrophic. Under pressure the board of the Group Theatre withdrew the play from rehearsal saying, "it is the policy of the Ulster Group Theatre to keep political and religious controversies off our stage".

James Ellis and Maurice O'Callaghan both resigned from the board in protest and their resignation was followed by that of Harold Goldblatt. Two producers from Dublin then stepped in to offer to finance a production of the play in the Grand Opera House. Eventually the actors supporting the play formed a new theatre company Bridge Productions and "Over the Bridge "played to a packed house in the Empire theatre on 26th January 1960.

Plays with an edgy focus on local problems were not the only ones to be treated with caution. In 1957 Tennessee Williams' play, "The Rose Tattoo" had been already banned in Dublin and its producer arrested The play was alleged to be an outrage to public morals. At the end of June it was to be performed in Belfast in the Grand Opera House. Two other controversial plays were already being staged in Belfast. John Osborne's, "Look Back in Anger" was at the Opera House and Arthur Millar's, "A View from the Bridge" was at the Arts. [Millar, a victim of the McCarthy witch hunts in America had just been convicted of contempt of Congress when he refused to name to McCarthy's Congressional Committee alleged communists known to him.]

Guardianship of public morals was taken very seriously. In 1950s Britain the usual procedure for not incurring charges of corrupting public morals was to submit the script to the Lord Chamberlain's Office which had the right to ban a play "The Rose Tattoo" was not vetoed for performance. An advisable next move was to consult the local police force in case local sensibilities could be offended.

In 1957 the Belfast Corporation Police Committee had banned the film, " Rock Around the Clock" on the grounds it was likely to cause a public disturbance and only after much debate agreed to another film, "Baby Doll" being shown to adults only audiences. So, the owner of the Grand Opera House, George Lodge, wisely gave the RUC copies of the script of "The Rose Tattoo" and allowed them to see a rehearsal.

The RUC saw nothing which could cause offence to the public and so Belfast was treated to a run of the play. Anyone who knows the play will agree that it is tame when compared to a week's run of "Eastenders" but it is a reflection of the times that it caused such a fuss in the Republic of Ireland and a closely run possible "no show" in the North.

If the delights on offer in Belfast were not enough for the culture vultures they could take the train South in May/June to the "an Tostal"- "Ireland's Springtime Festival". They could journey to Cork Opera House for an International Choral Festival or visit the George Bernard Shaw Centenary Season in the Olympia Theatre Dublin. An opera festival could be had at The Gaiety in Dublin and there was even a Mumming Festival at Rosslare Strand. All could be topped off by a visit to the Fleadh Cheoil na hEireann at Ennis, Co. Clare.

It's wonderful to look at what was on offer right across the arts before people were seduced by T.V.and the arts in general had to fight with the public for attention and the government for funding. It is obvious from surveying arts events available in the '50s that Belfast audiences were much more eclectic in composition than today and that Belfast people did not tolerate condescension nor expect their arts to be dumbed down and populist. They liked new plays; they did not shy from controversial ones; they attended concerts, exhibitions and theatrical events and made their own minds up. If you were no good they definitely let you know. If they liked your work you lived on in legend.

CHAPTER 9

THAT'S ENTERTAINMENT

The Pictures

I N THE EARLY '50s before the competition from T.V. really hit, people went to the cinema regularly.

Belfast was full of cinemas and as the decade went on and more and more of the population moved to the new suburbs new cinemas were built. A good example is the Lido Cinema on the Shore Road. When it opened in March 1955 it was the forty-fifth cinema in Belfast. It was a 1050 seater There was no balcony but the sloping floor allowed all patrons a good view of the specially installed latest wide -screen. The opening itself must have been really something. It was attended by the Lord Mayor of Belfast. The Faulet Girl Pipers marched in playing from the foyer and paraded down the centre aisle. There was a variety show starring the then up and coming comedian Frank Carson and the film was, "Take the Stage", a comedy western.

The programmes changed mid-week so cinema-goers sometimes went twice a week. Prices varied from1/= for the stalls to 2/6 for the gallery. For that money the cinema-goer expected a lot and got it. The normal programme consisted of ads for local businesses, trailers for "Coming Attractions", a Newsreel, "B" movie and a Main Attraction. In the Ritz Cinema there was all the added excitement and drama of a Wurlitzer organ emerging from the depths played by the virtuoso

Mr. Stanley Wylie. Everything was viewed through a haze of cigarette smoke.

Hollywood films predominated but British film makers did their best to keep up. For a grasp of what 1950s Britain was like it is worth a look at the films the Ealing Studios were producing at the time - many shot in Black and White. Post -war Britain provided the backdrop of classics like, "The Lavender Hill Mob", "Genevieve", "The Titfield Thunderbolt" and "Hue and Cry". Streets still had bombsites, there were not too many cars about, film stars were not botoxed and some like Alaistair Sim appeared to be seriously dentally challenged! The Britain portrayed in these films is also white and Anglo-Saxon.

Produced on both sides of the Atlantic were popular new genres like war films ["From Here to Eternity", "Stalag 17", "The Cruel Sea"] and sci-fi ["Them", "Forbidden Planet "and "Invasion of the Body Snatchers"]. American films also began to reflect the changing nature of society in the '50s with gritty realistic dramas like, "Blackboard Jungle" and "On The Waterfront".

But the real favourites were the big musicals and the "sand and sandals" epics.

Big films of the early '50s included that great homage to the arrival of talking pictures, "Singing in the Rain", fabulous musicals like "Bandwagon" and "Seven Brides for Seven Brothers", the ultimate in blarney, "The Quiet Man" and the "throw them to the lions" epic, "The Robe". To fend off the challenge from television, 1950s pictures simply became more and more colourful and lavish. They were shot in Cinema -scope. 3D, Todd A-O, Vistavision and all- surround sound.

Unfortunately sometimes the special effects proved too much for the viewer as a review in a 1955 " Belfast Newsletter" of the epic "The Egyptian" shows. It was a cinema scope spectacular with a cast of hundreds and very lavish sets. But the reviewer noted," for though the actors strive valiantly they are stifled by the magnificence of the effects".

People have very fond memories of the experience of cinema going in the '50. If the film was a blockbuster you joined a queue which was shepherded and controlled by a commissionaire resplendent in full uniform and peaked cap. Sometimes there were two queues one for the stalls and one for the balcony. On entering the foyer you paid your money at the ticket desk and might catch a glimpse of the manager. He was expected to look the part in a dinner jacket and bow tie. It all created the illusion that you were going somewhere really special. Cinema- goers then as now appeared to want to eat non-stop. A kiosk in the foyer would sell all kinds of sweets and quarter pound boxes of "Milk Tray" and "Black Magic" were much favoured by courting couples.

Once inside, the interior varied from the plush to the absolutely seedy depending on the age of the cinema. The "Curzon" on the Ormeau Road was the last word in plushness with its chic art deco interior and wide screen shielded by crimson velvet curtains Different coloured lights played on the closed curtains giving a borealis effect which was wonderful to behold. At the Interval in would come the ice cream girl and a queue would patiently form to buy tubs, choc ices or ice lollies. Sales of these could soar if the manager turned up the heat while showing a sand and sandals epic featuring a lot of desert. At the end of the evening a picture of the Queen on a horse in her Trooping the Colour gear would be displayed and the National Anthem played – this was the signal for most of the audience to make a bolt for the exits.

There were suspicions that cinema was not good for children. At its annual conference in January 1955 the Irish National Teachers Organisation actually called for a ban on children attending cinema in school hours and after certain hours at night. The speaker proposing the ban said that "excessive visits " to the cinema, "with its emotionally exciting and vitiated atmosphere" were harmful to children. [Belfast Newsletter]

However, the very popular Children's Saturday Cinema Clubs were to be found at different cinemas in the city. Attendance at these was not for the faint hearted as half the audience turned up fully armed with six shooter cap guns to join in the fights in the cowboy films on screen. All local gangs attended the same cinema and a truce for the duration of the cinema club could not always be guaranteed. Any hootchy- smoochy love scenes on screen were a direct turn off to the viewers. Rioting could break out until the hero returned to the serious business of shooting or biffing somebody and juvenile cinema-goers could return to chewing their "Everlasting Strips" or sucking their Gob-stoppers. Controlling the juvenile mob was a nightmare for the staff. Once the lights went down the usherettes swept the rows of children with torch beams that would have done credit to searchlight crews in the Blitz. The ice -cream girl, besieged at the interval, took her life in her hands. Order was kept by the burly commissionaire or a terrier of an usherette arresting the miscreants and chucking them out. The ultimate sanction was to end the picture and put the lights up until everybody calmed down.

A typical programme on offer was a cartoon or two, an episode of "Abbot and Costello" or "The Three Stodgies", then the Interval. During the Interval there would be a competition to find the youngest or oldest viewer, or a talent competition or spot prizes. The Interval was followed by the serial.

Often these were as old as the hills with "Buck Rodgers" constantly being left in an awful fix by "Ming- The Merciless".

Then came the cowboy film. The best of these was the adventures of singing cowboy Roy Rodgers who with his wife Dale, horse Trigger and Alsatian dog, Rebel sorted out the bad guys every Saturday. This was good wholesome stuff that even the I.N.T.O. would approve of for at the end of each film Trigger knelt down and Roy led the juvenile audience in "The Cowboy Prayer" before he and Dale sang "Happy Trails to You " and rode off into the sunset.

Then, magic of magic in March 1954. Roy and Dale on their tour of Britain came to Belfast! They stayed at the Grand Central Hotel and hundreds of over excited children turned up outside hoping for a glimpse of their heroes. Rumour swept the city that Trigger had his own room in the hotel. But the truth was that though Roy and Dale had travelled by plane from Liverpool, Trigger had come on the

Stranraer boat and was stabled in Chichester Street. The next evening Roy and ensemble did their show at the Hippodrome. He rode Trigger on to the stage to great applause and backed by his singing group "The Whipporwills" sang a repertoire of cowboy songs. The "Newsletter" reviewer reported that Trigger was a star "he can add, subtract and divide; he danced and even threw kisses on this exit"! Somehow or other word went round that Roy was to ride Trigger up the Ormeau Road to the Curzon and crowds in expectation lined the route. Alas, they were to be disappointed but the whole event goes to show the popularity of the children's cinema clubs.

The T.V. challenge was soon to change all that for not even Roy Rodgers and Trigger could compete with U.T.V.'s "Robin Hood and His Merrymen" or "Wagon Train".

CHAPTER 10

SHOWBIZ, PUNCH-UPS AND IDEAL HOMES

I N FEBRUARY 1955 CHARLIE Chaplin sent a letter to the Empire
Theatre Belfast congratulating it on its Diamond Jubilee. In its
and his early days he had actually appeared in the Empire. For a
full week the theatre celebrated with a sumptuous show which was
really a tribute to its past as a theatre of varieties. Marie Lloyd Jnr.
appeared and Lil O'Gorman led the audiences nightly with the songs
of music – hall favourite Florrie Ford. There was a comedian billed as
"Gumless and Gormless Bob Nelson", the Ken-Tones close harmony
group, the Patricia Mulholland Irish Dancers, jugglers, a medley of
musical impressions from The King Brothers and last but not least, a
contortionist, Eva May Wong. Variety shows were a regular feature of
Belfast entertainment with popular stars of the day and Belfast's own
local performers combining to give audiences a value for money night
out. Besides the Empire shows were to be found in Belfast in the Grand
Opera House, Ulster Hall and Royal Hippodrome Theatre.

A firm summer favourite with adults and children alike was
Chipperfield's Circus. The circus made an annual visit in June. For two
fabulous weeks in 1956 it raised its big tent, capable of seating 4000
people, on Cliftonville Football Ground and brought over to Belfast
in a specially chartered ship a tremendous menagerie of over 200
animals. There were elephants, chimps, Bengal tigers, lions, camels,
sealions, giraffes and a hippo. Even more remarkable was the inclusion
of 6 polar bears. The public was told that 72lbs of fresh herrings had
to be sourced every day just to feed the polar bears and the sealions.
Twenty-five tons of hay had to be found to feed other animals and

doubtlessly buckets upon buckets of bananas for the chimps!

When the circus opened extra police had to be drafted in to muster the eager crowd. In attendance were the Prime Minister of Northern Ireland and his wife, the Lord Mayor and Lady Mayoress of Belfast and guests. There was a delay of 15 minutes at the start of the show because all the people could not find their seats in time. Then the audience was treated to a two hour spectacular in which two elephants got a great cheer for performing a "Pride of Erin" waltz and George the giraffe graciously inclined his head to accept a chocolate from the hand of the PM's grandson.

Another visit of the circus in 1959 was memorable for two things- the parade of the circus animals up the Ormeau Road to Ormeau Park [that year's venue] and the attempt by one animal to eat somebody.

On 17th June a crowd of over 2000 children had waited at the dock gates at Whitla Street for the arrival of what the newspapers described as a "Noah's Ark" of circus animals. The children were to be disappointed as the ship did not make it into Belfast until 10pm by which time the children had been whisked home and tucked up in bed. But their disappointment was assuaged when it was announced that at 6.30pm on the 18th there would be a parade of animals led by the circus band to Ormeau Park. Crowds lined the route. It was like a scene from the popular children's T.V. programme "Circus Boy". Handlers rode the elephants mahout- style, the lion tamer cracked his whip, tumblers tumbled, the clowns charged about. The crowds loved it and cheered and applauded.

Who could resist making a visit to the circus after that?

The same night there was to be a charity performance at which the Prime Minister and his wife would be present. Everything went well until the crocodiles came on. Then in full view of the audience one of the crocs attacked its handler. It took a lump out of her and she had to be rushed to the RVH. She made a recovery and like a trooper went on with her act the next night. Noticeably no one wanted to occupy the seats nearest the ring in case the croc took a fancy to making another attempt to eat somebody.

Belfast had a great share of show-biz personalities. It had produced its own singing superstar Donegall Road girl, Ruby Murray. She had had considerable chart success beginning in December 1954 when her single, "Heartbeat" reached number 3 in the UK charts. This was followed in 1955 with another hit and the song everyone associates with Ruby Murray, "Softly, Softly". In fact 1955 was a huge year for her. She actually set a record by having five hit singles in the charts in the same week- something that was not to be equalled for years to come- Ruby appeared at the Royal Variety Show and did a world tour which included Belfast. Husky voiced Ruby appeared in the Hippodrome in July 1955. She was so overwhelmed by her home town welcome she broke down in tears. Her proud father watched the performance from a box and applauded her by waving his hat at the end of each number.

This was not to be Ruby's last time in Belfast. She returned again in 1956 to attend the wedding of her secretary Marie Cunningham in St. Patrick's Roman Catholic Church and was mobbed by well wishers. Each time Ruby Murray returned to her home town to make appearances she was always met with warmth and genuine affection.

Another star of the '50s with Belfast roots was Ronnie Carroll. Ronnie hailed from Roslyn Street in the Willowfield area of East Belfast. Ronnie Carroll had a pleasing mellow voice which was often compared to that of Nat King Cole When he made a personal appearance in Belfast in May 1956 the reviewer of his show complimented Carroll in not displaying the same awful mannerisms as other crooners!

It was not only home grown stars who visited Belfast.

The big children's film of 1956 was Walt Disney's, "Davy Crockett". Any self respecting junior would not be seen dead without a racoon hat. Imagine the delight when, in April, the actor playing Davy in the film, Fess Parker arrived to make a personal appearance in Belfast. But, on this visit Fess got more than he bargained for. On his way back to Nutt's Corner Miss Ethel Jenkins, a Queen's University student, lay down in the road in front of his car. When the car stopped and Parker got out to gentlemanly assist Miss Jenkins to her feet he found himself surrounded by "Red Indians" who had appeared as if out of nowhere. It was a stunt pulled by Queen's students as part of Rag Week- an innocent piece of fun involving no drink, police riot squads or any of the usual things students seem to attract nowadays. No-one was scalped, Fess handed over money for a copy of "Pro Tanto Quid" and was allowed to go on his way unharmed.

The arrival in Britain in 1957 of rock and roller Bill Haley and his band the Comets caused near riots wherever they appeared. Rock and Roll mania swept the country and eventually swept poor Ruby's gentle style of singing off the air. On 7th June in the Ulster Hall a crowd of 1500 roared with laughter at the sight of 12 people hypnotised by Edwin Heath on stage gyrating to rock and roll music.

Then in March, Haley visited Belfast on his British tour appearing at the Hippodrome. Signal a riot!. Unlike those of more recent times this one was not sectarian but was between gangs of "Teddy Boys" who had gathered outside the Hippodrome.

For good measure the crew of a Canadian naval vessel on leave in the town, taking umbrage at some cat-calling by the "Teds" joined in. A crowd of over 1000 had gathered outside the theatre chanting, "We want Bill" and when told by the police through loud hailers that Bill had long gone home the mob began to beat all round it. The RUC, no shrinking violets, waded in with batons to break up the running fights that then developed in Donegall Place. A pitched battle was fought in Royal Avenue in front of the GPO with the police as "piggy-in-the-middle". Naturally arrests were made!

Other big names appearing in Belfast had varying effects on fans. At the end of March 1957 TV glamour girl, Sabrina, made a personal appearance to open the Alpha Cinema in Rathcoole. She was met with flashing light bulbs and polite applause. In contrast the visit of another glamour puss in the same month, blonde bombshell, Diana Dors caused another near riot. She with her famous platinum barnett came to open the new hairdressing salon in Robb's. Traffic came to a standstill in Castle Junction as the crowd pressed all around the outside of the store for a glimpse of the film star. Screams went up as a big car was seen inching its way towards the front door. The car was a ruse as Diana Dors had already been spirited in to the building through the side door in Lombard Street. However, shrewdly aware of the opportunity for publicity, Diana clad in a clinging black suit and swathed in a silver mink stole made an appearance at a first floor window and waved and blew kisses to the ecstatic fans below.

Cordons of police had to hold back hysterical female fans when crooner Frankie Vaughan came to open the Gaiety Supermarket in Upper North Street in June '57. When he gave his trade mark high kick several women overcome by the near presence of their idol fainted.

Another really big name appearing in Belfast was Cary Grant who came to promote a film. The debonair Grant made a big impact strolling about the stage of the Ritz Cinema politely and good humouredly answering questions on his career and latest film. Tommy Steele appeared and had the same rock and roll effect as Bill Haley but threatened not to play if fans did not calm down. The legendary American singer Paul Robson also came and got a great reception from Belfast audiences.

A big name of a different kind visited the city in March 1959. Sir John Betjeman gave a talk to a packed Whitla Hall at Queen's on the work of the National Trust. He spoke generously of the architecture of Belfast and grew ever more rapturous about the Victorian glories of the GNR, St.Anne's, the buildings of central Belfast and even the Gas Works. He described Elmwood Presbyterian Church as "byzantine" and loved the fine Italinate styling of the Provincial Bank, the Central library and the Water Office. Praise was given to the "Swiss-style" book stalls of York Street Station and he pronounced the Crown Bar as "a superb example of the old gin palace." Concluding his talk Sir John warned Ulster to guard against ugly modernisation. It is a pity no one listened.

Another annual favourite was the "Ideal Home Exhibition" at the King's Hall. In 1958 it was in its twenty-third year and the winning formula for attracting crowds was set. Every show had a Show House. In '58 it was a timber framed house with a brick "veneer". Of course it sported all the latest mod-cons such as a car port which could double as an outdoor lounge in summer, timber floors an open plan living room and a ducted warm-air central heating system throughout. The exhibitor assured you that a similar luxury ideal home could be built for you at £2,400. Queues to see inside the Ideal Home often stretched around the ground floor of the hall such was the interest in it.

A report in the "Belfast Newsletter" in November 1959 suggests that the interest in seeing the latest designs in homes was not confined to the once yearly exhibition. People living on new estates reported that they were fed up with their areas being invaded on Sundays by sight seers who walked up and down and unashamedly peered at the house and through the very windows.

Other regular features of the exhibition were cookery demonstrations, fashion shows, talent competitions and all the latest gadgets. If you had made your way to Stands 119-120 you could have tried all the latest Singer Sewing machine models. Brooke Bond Tea was on Stands 106-107 and the National Bank was willing to provide "a full banking service for customers and exhibitors" at Stands 123-124. If you had wanted a sit down then the places to go were the Fashion Theatre to see the show and also to listen to Ivy Benson and her Band or to Ulster's Own Ideal Home Economic Kitchen to see a cookery demonstration by Mrs. H. P. Moore and her team of demonstrators. Inevitably a visit to the show resulted in the purchase of some daft gadget sold by a silver tongued salesperson and quickly relegated to the back of a kitchen cupboard after a short period of use. The Ideal Home Exhibition was a favourite with women. Some Belfast men preferred their entertainment to carry a bit more of a punch.

The Ulster Hall and King's Hall were the venues for Boxing. Sometimes the crowd angered by the result of a bout was not averse to a bit of an argy -bargy itself. One contest which got out of hand happened at the King's hall in February 1956. Billy Kelly a fighter from L'Derry lost his British Featherweight title to Charlie Hill [Glasgow]. The Belfast crowd did not agree with the verdict. Chairs and bottles were soon being hurled from all directions. Though the Referee got away without being injured the Match Compeer was felled by a flying chair and three other ringside officials were also casualties. Hill and his seconds just made it to their dressing room by the skin of their teeth. It took half an hour to restore order and then the evening actually proceeded. The boxers coming out for the rest of the bouts must have felt it was like entering the Roman arena.

The Ulster Hall was in the '50s and is still essentially a concert hall. Under the control of the Belfast Corporation it could not make a profit.

My Fights and Follies

BY

RINTY MONAGHAN

START ON SUNDAY
in the

SUNDAY DISPATCH

The hall had become a bit down at heel - one councillor not mincing his words described it as "a dirty, drab dismal-looking hole". The hall was incurring a loss of £1500 per year so, after a heated debate in July 1956, it was decided by 15-10 to allow it to become a venue for boxing.

During the debate the point had been made that if the Ulster Hall was given over to other things Belfast needed a proper purpose built civic concert hall. Alderman Tommy Henderson, the ever vocal self appointed champion of the working man then pronounced that, "It was only funny fellows like the Philharmonic who wanted a civic hall." Belfast people he stated were not much interested in classical music preferring as he put it, "the big drum". The debate about a civic hall was to rattle on for decades.

During "The Troubles" Belfast was starved of big names too concerned with their own safety to play to audiences here or who considered Belfast too provincial.

What a contrast the 1950s had been to that.

CHAPTER 11

HOLIDAYS

OFF TO THE SEASIDE—Mothers and babies of Ariel Street Baby Club photographed at the Maternity and Child Welfare Clinic prior to leaving for their annual outing to Bangor yesterday.

J UST BEFORE THE OUTBREAK of the Second World War the Holidays With Pay Act had been passed at Westminster. This enabled most people to take at least a week's holiday from work usually during the "Twelth Week" in July. The average wage in 2010-2011 is around £538 per week for men and £439 per week for women. In the 1950s the mostly male workforce averaged between £8-10 for blue collar workers and £14 per week for white collar workers. Even with a paid week's leave the 1950s family found holidays expensive.

So, many firms had holiday clubs where a bit of money could be put aside each week out of wages to pay for the holiday. Money could also be laid aside for holiday essentials and shoe and clothing clubs also existed. There was a sort

of summer uniform to be paid for and adhered to. Fathers wore blazers or sports jackets, "flannels", open neck shirts and sandals with socks. Mothers wore summer dresses with an obligatory "Banlon" cardigan. Youngsters were very often head to toe in Ladybird tee -shirts, jumpers and slacks or shorts. An industrious mother would have spent the best part of the winter knitting summer cardigans and pullovers. Summer sandals for all were de rigor and there was even a year when plastic sandals for children became a fashionable alternative to the usual "Startrite" leather ones and youngsters' feet sweated in the heat.

Prices for foreign travel were well beyond the means of the average person who had to content themselves with more home grown holidays. The norm for families was a "day here and there – a train or bus to Bangor, Portrush or Newcastle or an adventurous excursion on one of the UTA's "Mystery Trains". These trains usually ended up in Bundoran which suited well since in the early '50s with rationing in full swing in the North many things on ration could be freely had south of the border. So, for the majority of working class families a good week off could consist of a visit to the seaside, a day at the zoo and a trip to the cinema.

Belfast Corporation had in 1910 acquired the Cavehill and Whitewell Tramway Company along with 40 acres of grounds at Bellevue. These pleasure grounds eventually contained a Golf Course, Putting Green, Dance Hall [the famed Floral Hall], Barry's Amusements, a boating lake and of course, the Zoo.

The Zoo was not without its detractors. In 1954 a debate had arisen over conditions for the animals on what the Secretary of the Cats' Protection League described as "a bitter slope". During the debate a city councillor said that the zoo was a miserable and unhappy place for the animals and the Dean of Belfast pleading for improvements to be made added,

"Animals from the forest in captivity behind bars in a small area is contrary to decency."

The recently setup Zoological Society argued that the zoo should remain open but be improved and so it was.

During the Easter Break and the summer holidays Bellevue Zoo was a magnet for families. On Easter Monday 1956, undeterred by any concerns voiced about animal welfare, an estimated 100,000 people passed through the gates of Bellevue and 150 children in the course of the day had been lost and found. The bus service could hardly cope with the crowds queuing for buses out to and back from the zoo. Favourites with the children were the elephant, the seals and penguins, Children's Corner where children could stroke small domestic animals like rabbits. A firm favourite was Peter the Polar Bear. Today Peter can be viewed stuffed at the Ulster Museum in Belfast!

A day at the seaside took a lot of planning. Anyone who thinks the summers were always warmer then needs only to glance at family photos taken on a seaside trip. All the adults wrapped up in Aran sweaters and wool coats and the children shivering in ruched bathing suits. Grandfather in full three piece suit plus cap; Granny swathed in a wool coat and in inclement weather with a "Rainmate" on her head to protect her perm. Only a fool ventured far without a "Pacamac" raincoat to hand.

As eating out on day trips would be expensive, families travelled with large thermos flasks with a bung replacing the now more familiar screw top. The grease- proof paper in which a loaf of bread had been wrapped was saved and then used to wrap the sandwiches and any home- made buns. The wrapped sandwiches etc were then carried in an empty biscuit tin. Milk was in a lemonade bottle with a screw top or the original milk bottle. Some adventurers even possessed a little Primus stove which worked on mentholated spirits. Everything was placed in a large shopping bag and off the family went like an expedition to Equatorial Africa.

August 1952 was an absolute wash out. Freak floods destroyed the town of Lynmouth in Devon and 36 people died. On 10th August at 3pm a downpour began in Belfast and continued until noon the next day drowning 100 acres of the city to a depth of four feet. The Blackstaff River broke its banks and flood water rushed down Tate's Avenue and the Donegall Road. One elderly resident at 100 Benburb Street was marooned upstairs for ten hours before being rescued. In just twenty-four hours nearly the average rainfall for the whole of August had cascaded from the skies. People sought reassurance that this weather had nothing to do with the testing of H-bombs!

In contrast, the summer of 1954 was an absolute scorcher. People

flocked to the city's parks for picnics and to the seaside. People drank so much lemonade that it had to be rationed and the demand for ice lollipops outstripped supply. Crisis confronted the city's dairies - they ran out of milk bottles. Families had gone off on day trips with milk bottles and then discarded the empties

This sand-castle at Bangor looked as if it might remain a "castle in the air" until Father came to the rescue. But, one of the builders still looks rather dubious.

Dry cleaners were swamped with orders for cleaning light-weight clothes and eventually there was not a pair of sandals to be had for love or money in the whole of Belfast.

That same year on Saturday 9th July, the first day of the "Twelth Holidays" 50,000 left Belfast by bus, train, private car or boat. The Bangor Road was congested from 3.30pm until 4.30pm and the number of passengers carried the next day by train was 15,000.

Those not on day trips were heading off to boarding houses, houses or wooden bungalows rented for their holiday. Bangor is now a commuter town for Belfast so we perhaps do not appreciate the attraction it held for the 1950s visitor.

As boarding houses more or less locked guests out from dawn to dusk it was important that a resort like Bangor offered a full day of activity. There was Picky Pool – an outdoor swimming pool with water colder than the North Atlantic. In the evenings Square dancing was held in the area adjacent to the pool and hundreds of visitors went. For children there was not only the beach but also Barry's Amusements.

A gruesome lot, 1950s children enjoyed the penny slot machines showing a bizarre collection of executions –"The Electric Chair", "The Guillotine". There was also "The House on Fire" [basically a big doll's house with artificial flames created by painted pieces of cardboard shooting up and down at the windows and doors], "What the Butler Saw" [very tame], "The Fortune Teller" [a dummy wearing a turban dispatching for the princely sum of two pence pasteboard cards with your "fortune" on them] the usual jumble of shove happenny and one armed bandits and last but not least, The Dodgems.

An alternative entertainment was Gypsy Lee who advertised foretelling the future by reading palms. He must have alerted himself to the prospect of a bad season in 1955 because he decided in August to abandon fortune telling in favour of attracting a big crowd by turning evangelist. Riding a pony along the sea front he sported a jumper with the words," I'm saved. Are You?" emblazoned on the front. He then told the waiting crowd he intended to give up the palm reading and chuck away his crystal ball. To the disappointment of the crowd which had hoped to see the crystal ball hurled dramatically into the sea he reneged at the last minute and just burnt some astrological charts. Ostentatiously blessing the bemused spectators he then about turned the pony and rode off. Still, it made a difference to square dancing.

An alternative to the boarding house was to hire a wooden bungalow. On the Down coast these were to be found on the Donaghadee High Road, along the road from Groomsport where some survivors can still be glimpsed and at Millisle and Ballywhisken. Forerunners of the much more sophisticated static caravan they were very basic with a small living area and perhaps two bed rooms. Cooking was done over a gas stove or a small range. Sadly in 1957 a gassing tragedy occurred in a bungalow on the Clandeboye Road in Bangor resulting in the distressing deaths of five children from an East Belfast family.

Northern Ireland's seaside resorts thrived in the 1950s not only because of local patronage but also because of an annual invasion of Scottish visitors. During Glasgow Fair Week up 20,000 made the journey from Scottish industrial towns via the Glasgow, Ardrossan or Heysham boats. Special extra trains and buses had to be laid on to convey this horde from the docks to the resorts and boarding houses which were full from the last week in July to the end of August.

"Norn Iron Speak" may have held no mysteries for the lowland Scots but English holiday-makers could find local idiom perplexing. One Englishman was baffled as to why a fishmonger standing beside a box of obviously dead fish was shouting, "Herrens Alive!" With unflinching Ulster logic the fishmonger told him that the fish were so fresh that if they were in the sea instead of the box they would still be swimming!

Those Belfast people with a "roughness" of money could plan on a holiday out of Northern Ireland. There was after all the lure of the Republic of Ireland's resorts where unlike the north some things might be open on Sundays. In May 1953 a tempting advert appeared in the "Irish News" –

"Irish holiday now and enjoy yourself among friends. You can choose just the type of holiday you want- gay* restful or energetic."

[*It is remarkable the change in meaning this word has undergone since the '50s. In another glorious incidence from the "Belfast Newsletter" there is the joyful caption to a photograph –"Tram goes gay for driver's last trip"]

The UTA offered bus tours south of the border from York Street Station. You could go to Buncrana for 21/6 or the more flush with money could have a four day trip to Connemara for 13 Guineas.

For anyone wanting their entertainment organised on a non-stop basis Butlin's at Moseley beckoned. It even held a grand reunion dance each January in The Orpheus Ballroom, Belfast.

Of course you could always drive yourself about Ireland on a touring holiday if you could afford to. For under £500 anyone could buy a Ford Popular and for between £500 and £700 a Morris Minor, Austin A35 or even a Hillman Minx. By 1956 there were 80,000 licensed vehicles in Ulster. Unfortunately cruising about in private cars was curtailed by the Suez Crisis of 1956 and the reintroduction of petrol rationing.

Holiday-makers to the mainland usually travelled by sea on the British Railways Packet Steamers to Heysham or Liverpool.

BRITISH RAILWAYS' STEAMERS
THE CORONATION
TUESDAY, 2nd JUNE, 1953
SPECIAL SAILING BELFAST TO HEYSHAM
10-30 p.m., SUNDAY, MAY 31st
With through train connection to LONDON. *Early Booking Advisable.*
BRITISH RAILWAYS, 24, Donegall Place, BELFAST

To make sure of having a berth at times of high demand for the overnight crossing everyone had to have a sailing ticket.

People actually queued from midnight on 2nd January until opening time the next morning at the British Rail Office at 9 Donegall Street to make sure of these.

Failure to secure a berth meant sitting up all night in the open space accommodation on board. Not a good prospect for a family with small children. Those securing berths found the cabins outfitted in mahogany [not a piece of MDF in sight] and the berths equipped with stiff cotton sheets and blankets with the Steam Packet logo stamped on them. The Irish Sea was seldom calm and rounding the Calf of Man was as dreaded as going around Cape Horn in a Force 8.

You would assume that those with the most money could get the furthest away on holiday but even those better off were a bit restricted with their holiday plans.

Though you could book for exotic climes until 1957 you could only take £25 spending money out of the country.

By 1952 British European Airways was trying to get around this currency restriction by offering holidays abroad with a shrewd calculation built in of how much spending money you would need.

The price included flight from Belfast, hotel, all meals and tips.

For example, flying from Belfast to Paris for five days would cost £31 with the promise that the holiday maker would only need to take £18 spending money. An all in deal for eight days in Switzerland was priced at £49 with a guarantee that you would only need an allowance of £15 spending money. The currency restriction was eventually eased in 1957 allowing those with the means and a sense of adventure to venture further afield to the USA or Canada. A flight from London to New York cost £151 and the more luxurious crossing on a Cunard liner [tourist return] was priced at £128.11.5.

For reading material on the voyage travellers could do worse than choose from the many self-improvement books advertised by Erskine Mayne's:

- How to Read Hands
- The Art of Relaxed Living
- Understanding Nervous Disorders and Hysteria
- Better Eyesight Without Glasses

The sophisticated few who experienced foreign travel brought home with them a taste for foreign food so SD Bell's of 63 Ann Street began importing exotic fare. From Italy came Salami, Ravioli and Italian Tomato products, from France rarities like Pate de Foie Gras, Dijon Mustard and Escargots and from Germany, Anchovy Paste and Frankfurters. Even more exotic yearnings could be catered for by the new Turkish Baths just opened at Pakenham Street by well known local physio – Thomas Grant.

These were bang up to date with radiant heat baths, a Turkish bath heated to 180C of dry heat and a Russian bath with humid heat of 150C. There was also a massage room and a lounge where the client could get just the very thing to top off their visit - a cup of tea.

At the other end of the scale what did the poorer citizens of Belfast do for a holiday? Generally they sat tight at home or relied on free trips and charity.

The Shankill Road Mission ran a Holiday Home in Bangor for needy mothers and children. In 1952 the Superintendent, Rev. Andrew McNab, estimated that over the 53 years that the mission had been in operation 50,000 children had had their lives enriched by the mission's work. Much good work was also done by the Grosvenor Hall which ran Childhaven in Millisle. Then there were the days out of the Sunday School Trips and those of the Mothers and Babies' clubs.

A favourite venue for these day trippers was Helen's Bay beach. In 1955 organisers of outings for deprived children had taken 700 for the day to this beach. They hoped to double this in 1956. But, the owners of the beach, the Clandeboye Estate threatened this plan by intending to make money out of the beach. They actually closed it off with barbed wire; a turnstile was installed and charges imposed of 1/= for adults and 6d for children. Season tickets could be had for £1. Locals and day-trippers alike were furious and vowed to mass trespass if necessary to regain entry to the beach.

Lastly, the holiday maker absent from home for the day or the week had to be vigilant about securing their empty property. In June 1956 the "Newsletter" reported a spate of burglaries in the new houses at Glengormley. The robbers were pretty cool customers. When they broke into a local chippy they had calmly helped themselves to lemonades and biscuits and they outfitted themselves from head to toe when they burgled a local clothes shop. At least the police knew the sizes of the burglars they were hunting. The thieves crowned all when they removed a front window of a house and robbed the house while the family slept the sleep of the dead upstairs.

Holiday makers fear of burglars probably accounted for why on locking the front door prior to setting off my mother then shoulder charged it and half way to the destination ruined my father's holiday by asking, "Did you make sure the back door was locked?"

CHAPTER 12

TAKE ME TO YOUR LEADER!

THE '50S SAW THE beginning of our fascination with- "is anybody out there?" Films of the day reflect this with the arrival of a new genre - Sci-fi Cinema audiences paid up to be terrified by "Invasion of the Body-Snatchers" and "The Thing from Outer Space". Newspapers regularly carried stories from around the world about UFOs and alien invaders.

One such tale was that of the disappearing hose pipe of Mr. George di Peso of Downey California. Mr. di Peso watched as his hose was drawn mysteriously down into the earth at a rate of 2-3 inches per hour by a mysterious force. Crowds came from far and near to witness the event. One woman terrified the di Peso family by turning up at dead of night with a flashlight. The di Pesos thought aliens had landed. Eventually Mr. di Peso could stand no longer the crowd of locals invading his garden on a daily basis and took a pair of shears to the offending hosepipe.

Another story carried by local papers concerned the alleged sighting by a French farmer living in deepest France of two types of alien invaders. The first type was tall and wore a sort of grey lycra outfit and elongated cycling helmet. On sighting the farmer this alien had scarpered. The second type was short and after kissing the farmer on both cheeks had made off in a small cigar shaped space craft. The local mayor when questioned said insanity had run in the farmer's family!

Both stories illustrate how credulous the public is about the possibility that "we are not alone". On 5th September 1956 Belfast even had its own sighting of a U.F.O hovering over Stormont! Local residents had watched strange lights in the sky for over two hours. Was it a trick of the light, a weather balloon released from Aldergrove, a reflection of the red lights atop the radar masts at Dundonald ? Or, was it spacemen looking at our spacers in the Stormont Parliament?

Both the U.S. and U.S.S.R. claimed that they would soon be able to create rockets powerful enough to launch satellites into orbit around the earth. In a propaganda war against each other they also said space travel to the Moon and the further exploration of planets would become a possibility within a decade.

In June 1957 an insurance company had actually agreed to insure a woman waiting on the possibility of a flight to Mars. The insurers had the good sense to insert a special clause – "Non-return is no proof of death". There were reports of people putting down their children's names for flights to the moon in case the possibility of going there came too late for them.

Then in October 1957 came Sputnik. The USSR succeeded in launching a satellite which was orbiting the earth at 18,000mph at a height of 560 miles. The Russians were very cagey about what this satellite could do. This was the height of the Cold War. Ulster had already played its part in sheltering Hungarians fleeing their home land in the aftermath of the Hungarian Rising, 1956. The U.S. USSR and Britain had all tested hydrogen bombs. Belfast newspapers regularly carried adverts urging people to join their local Civil Defence Corps. Those volunteering were equipped with a greatcoat and a button-hole badge and some were armed. Everyone must have rested easier in their beds knowing they were so well defended from H-Bombs!

Was this flying pressure cooker, Sputnik, sending back pictures of strategic US defences? What were the coded signals it was transmitting? Professor Meessel, Professor of Physics at Sydney University did not mince his words –

"this means life or death for us – freedom or the extinction of civilisation."

For Ronald Fails, assistant science teacher at Linfield Secondary School Belfast it meant great excitement and a moment of fame. Mr.Fails was one of the first people to pick up the signal from Sputnik. He did so whilst tuning his TV set to a signal lower than that transmitted by the Divis transmitter. On October 28th Sputnik was over Belfast and in the clear weather it was visible to the many watching below.

In November, the Russians followed up the success of Sputnik by launching Sputnik 2 containing a dog called, Laika. Instead of engendering more fear about the possible strategic weapon use of the satellite this produced outraged protests from animal lovers all over the world. On 4th November Laika was over Belfast when Mr.Fails did it again and picked up the signal. Dog lovers had been furious with Radio Tangier which had broadcast a spoof interview with the dog.

In reply to questions such as, "Are you proud of being the first living thing to travel in space?" and "What would you like to do when you get back?" Laika had apparently obliged by woofing. Mr Fails did not report picking up any woofs.

On 11th November an Italian newspaper reported that to be spared the pain of re-entry Laika had been poisoned by its last mouthful of food. Moscow refused to confirm this. Dog lovers mourned. Letters of complaint were delivered to the Russian embassy in London.

The efforts to put man on other planets and its collision with the world of sci-fi produced a few interesting spin offs. One was the invention of aluminium foil and a serious proposal in 1959 that it would become the material of the future for clothes. Anything from boiler suits to evening dresses could be created using this new shimmering foil which would keep you warm in winter and cool in summer. One big drawback however was that the foil did not allow perspiration to evaporate. So the dream of wearing it as the spacemen did in the sci-fi films faded. But today any visit to a Space Science Museum will reveal what a vital material the foil actually did become for space travel.

Another spin off was surely a fascination with weird science. In the shoe departments of Tyler's Shoes and the Cooperative Store Belfast there was a machine which could X-ray feet to check on the fit of shoes. Anyone standing on the machine could look through a screen and see their toes wiggling. It was like something seen only in "Flash Gordon" films and children were fascinated by it. So much so that the Medical Research Council of Great Britain actually said that multiple exposures were dangerous and the possibility of radiation from these machines was greater than that of atomic bomb tests. If only my mother had known!

For people who had come through the devastation of a World War just 10-15 years previously and still had the scars of blitzed sites in their town this brave new world of H-Bombs, space travel and a Cold War must at times have created great anxiety. Not surprising then that people found the possibility that Ulster would acquire an atomic power station to generate its electric power something to worry about.

This was announced in March 1957 by Lord Glentoran. The proposed site was somewhere around Lough Neagh. Trigger protests from terrified locals and reassurances from the Stormont government that such stations were absolutely safe.

But Ulster was in the midst of a sustained IRA campaign - what if they blew up part of an atomic power plant? Locals were not to be placated. In the end the plan was shelved cutting short a new version of Bill Haley's, "See you later alligator". With typical Belfast humour this had become- "See you later generator – In a while atomic pile."

CHAPTER 13

TOYS

I
N NOVEMBER 1958 ANDERSON and MacAuley's ran a children's competition which was sponsored by MacDonald's biscuits. The eight winners were to be given the freedom of the store's Toy Department and in a ten minute snatch and grab to pick as many toys as they liked. The children managed to clean the store out of the considerable sum of £1031 worth of toys.

There were different age categories of winners ranging from 7-14 years old. Would any of today's fourteen year olds even enter such a competition which did not include designer gear? The youngest winners were Mary Bell [7 years] and Robert McCoy [8 years]. They were allotted the full ten minutes whereas the eldest two who were fourteen years old, Simon Peter Swan and Adelaide Campbell, got only five minutes each. One boy, eleven year old Michael Fitzpatrick of Sicily Park Belfast selflessly chose toys not only for himself but also for his brothers and sisters. He netted a haul worth £247 in just eight minutes. He grabbed a Meccano set, a train set, tennis and badminton racquets, bicycles, tricycles and a doll's pram.

Michael's choices reflect the child's world of the 1950s. In an age before I-Pad2s, X-Boxes, Nintendos and other electronic gadgets needing only the movement of thumbs the 1950s youngsters' toys were tools to spark the imagination of children who played outdoors and with others. This is not to say that the '50s were not without crazes a great many of which were imported from the USA. Whole streets could be taken over by hip swivelling Hula Hoop-ers or twirling YoYo-ers who had temporarily abandoned skipping or French cricket. My father who was up a ladder painting the outside of the house once witnessed three small boys wearing Davy Crockett hats panther crawl up the street towards a workman who was just emerging from a manhole cover. Before he could shout a warning to the unfortunate man the leading would be frontiers-man had reversed the butt of his gun and clobbered the fellow.

Walt Disney had a lot to answer for. Besides Davy Crockett ["King of the Wild Frontier"] hats Disney merchandise was taking off in the '50s. Plastic Snow White figurines, Pluto toys with wind up tails, Mickey and Minnie Mouse dolls were much desired. Indeed, besides Disney, the cinema had a lot to do with the toys children wanted and would weave games around. Cowboy and Cowgirl suits, silver six-guns in mock leather holsters, pop-gun rifles, guns with exploding caps were de rigor for those who charged about the streets mimicking their screen idols and slapping their sides to urge on imaginary horses. Some unfortunates got Red Indian outfits and were perpetually cast in the role of "baddies" perhaps because the outfit contained a bow and arrows which even with rubber stickers on the end could put an eye out. Do I hear you mutter, "Health and Safety"? Sorry, no such thing.

Parents who were aspirational for their offspring preferred to invest in dress up costumes of another kind. Doctors' and Nurses' outfits with hard shell plastic doctor's bag complete with enough plastic stethoscopes, thermometers, scissors, scalpels and bandages to treat all kinds of unwitting patients. For the would-be entrepreneur there was a toy Post Office or Sweet Shop. The Post Office and Sweet Shop had everything in miniature, little pieces of paper and envelopes, stamps and postal orders, tiny bottles of favourite sweets like Dolly Mixtures and Brandy Balls. Needless to say the Sweet Shop ran out of stock quickly.

Boys loved the engineering puzzles of putting together Meccano models. The Meccano set came with numerous metal parts which could be locked together with tiny screws and bolts to make bridges, cars, aeroplanes and all manner of marvels. It only took ingenuity and perhaps the help of an older brother or a father. The would-be model maker also could buy Airfix kits and make replica models of ships and military and civilian aircraft. Just add imagination and battle could commence. With memories of World War 2 still very clear a great deal of boys' play and comics were given over to an "Us versus The Gerries" storyline. One newspaper actually gave out the instructions for building your own firing range with pop up targets of heads at which you could fire your airgun!

When not mucking about with model building, glue and air guns boys could set up endless games of the comparatively civilised Subbuteo football. You could create a team with all your favourite players and take on all comers. Hornby train sets were the desire of many a small boy. These were beautifully crafted with the engines being to scale replicas of actual trains. It was not enough to have the train and track. To gain real kudos and the admiration of pals toy trees, tunnels, a station, signal box and miniature figures would have to be added. Hours would then be spent on imaginary journeys. Grown men still do this!

The 1950s was not a decade of equality between the sexes so girls' toys reflected the role they would be expected to fulfil - that of wife and mother. Girls played with dolls. They washed them, dressed them in elaborate outfits [there were knitting patterns for clothes for the doll], put them in prams which were replicas of the "Cross" pram or "Tansads" [the buggy of the day] and took them for walks. It was not unusual to come across a dolls' tea party; prams parked, dolls and owners clustered on a rug using miniature tea sets and pouring imaginary tea out of a tea pot whilst conversing like their elders. Often the party would be broken up by the mimicked arrival of "father" home from work and the tea things would be put away and the visitors and dolls dismissed. All observed from real life or gleaned from the "Janet and John" series of children's books? These children's reading books emphasised strongly the stereotypical roles of the parents in the family. Toy cosmetic sets, sewing kits and dressing table sets of plastic combs and brushes were the bane of many a girl's life when she would have preferred Spirograph or a tin robot with flashing eyes and ray gun to play with.

Everyone who was a child in the '50s will have a favourite memory of a loved toy or game - many of them very simple things like: pierry and whip, jacks, marbles, spinning top, Mr Potato Head, a spud gun, a golliwog [nowadays not very PC] a Sooty puppet, toy piano, tin rocket or American police car complete with siren, a scooter or, skates. The toy museums are full of examples of them and of adults pointing, laughing and remembering the fun, the games, the friends and being chased by neighbours who had had enough of cricket balls or footballs banging off gable walls or endless noise from the games being played outside. In the future will people feel the same about computer games and will they have had the same richness of imagination and social experience - I wonder.

CHAPTER 14

INTRIGUE AND TRAGEDIES

November 1952 - The Scandal of the Whiteabbey Murder.

THE 1952 MURDER OF 19 year old Patricia Curran, daughter of Mr. Justice Lancelot Curran, caused a sensation at the time and continues to be something which intrigues many today. Why? Maybe because it remains unsolved but then, so do many of Northern Ireland's recent murders. Maybe because it has been suggested that some kind of cover up was going on. There has been the suggestion of a conspiracy by the great and good of the 1950s Unionist hierarchy. In reconstructions it is presented in a film noir way with emphasis on the wind and the rain in the trees on the night of the murder; the dripping, dank darkness of that long tree lined driveway up to the Curran house, The Glen.

Whatever the reasons the mix of judge's allegedly promiscuous daughter, Ulster high society, suspected cover up and the violence of the crime are what seem to contribute to the interest in this case which caused a sensation at the time.

What are the beginnings of the story?

13th November 1952, 2.20 a.m, the body of Patricia Curran was carried into the surgery of Dr. Kenneth Wilson by two men – Desmond Curran, Barrister at Law, the girl's 25 year old brother and Malcolm Davidson, the Curran family solicitor. Dr Wilson, the Curran family doctor examined the body. The girl was dead and such was the pattern of wounds on the body he concluded that cause of death was that she had been sprayed with pellets from a shotgun. Dr Wilson on the basis of the rigor mortis of the body pronounced that Patricia had been dead four or five hours. In actual fact, the pathologist flown in from Preston the next day identified that she had been the subject of a frenzied attack with a thin bladed knife and sustained 37 stab wounds. There were no signs of stab wounds on her arms or hands leading to the conclusion that she had not had time to defend herself. The pathologist Dr Firth said she could have been killed at any time up to midnight.

The frenzied attack sent shockwaves through the community and triggered a man-hunt for the perpetrator. Ultimately a young RAF man called Iain Hay Gordon was arrested and tried for the crime.

But the question which has continued to exercise minds is did Hay Gordon do it or was the 20 year old Scottish airman the victim of an elaborate cover up for the identity of the real killer. Gordon and his parents always maintained his innocence saying he had been bullied by Superintendent Capstick of Scotland Yard into making a confession to the crime.

Here is an extract from that confession which was written by Capstick and signed by Iain Hay Gordon:

"I struggled with her, and she said to me," Let me go or I will tell my father." I then lost control of myself and Patricia fell down on the grass, sobbing. She appeared to have fainted because she went limp. I am a bit hazy about what happened next, but I probably pulled the body of Patricia through the bushes to hide it."

On 6th March 1953 Gordon was pleaded "Not Guilty by reason of insanity". Judged guilty of the murder he was sentenced to be detained in Holywell mental hospital " at Her Majesty's pleasure."

On 20th December 2000 Lord Chief Justice Carswell overturned the conviction on the grounds that the confession was unsound.

This does not completely remove the possibility of Gordon being the murderer. But if he did not do it then who killed the 19 year old Queen's University Art student on her way home that dark wet winter evening?

To unravel this murder the facts need to be closely questioned. But sometimes what are presented as the facts are not what they seem and this has led some to believe that in the case of "The Whiteabbey Murder" as the Press called it there was a conspiracy to obscure the truth.

Here are the details garnered from the "Belfast Newsletter", "Irish News" and "Belfast Telegraph" reports at the time. Noting the times given is particularly important.

November 12th – the day of the murder.

The victim spent the day of 12th November in Belfast. She had arranged to play Squash with her then boyfriend, John Steele at the Queen's University courts at Sans Souci. The courts were overbooked so the two had to give this idea up. Patricia said she was tired anyway and she decided to go on home. Steele walked her to York Street Bus Station. There was time to spare so the couple went into the Sorrento Café leaving at 5pm. Patricia was laden down with her handbag, books, an art folder, an umbrella and a Squash racquet when she joined the queue for the bus. She was wearing a yellow Juliet cap. When she boarded her bus the station clock read 5pm. The clock was subsequently found to be running ten minutes slow. The bus therefore left the station at 5.10pm and reached Whiteabbey 40 minutes later [5.50pm].

Two eyewitness passengers said they saw Patricia get off the bus at her usual stop. Her normal routine because she hated the long walk up the dark drive was to phone for a lift up to the house. [If these facts are correct as she stands at the bottom of the driveway she could be just minutes from meeting her murderer.] The information from the Currans is that no one in the house took any phone call from Patricia and she never arrived home.

1.45 am November 13th. Constable Rutherford, RUC Duty Constable at Whiteabbey Police Station received a call from Mr. Justice Curran to say that his daughter had not come home. The Constable was asked to come up to The Glen. Before Rutherford could get his coat on and collect his bike another phone call came in. This time it was a woman's voice, "Something awful has happened......" The phone line went dead. Rutherford said he thought someone had suddenly cut the connection. There is speculation by the conspiracy theorists that the second caller was Mrs. Curran.

Constable Rutherford cycled to the house and was met in the driveway by Mr. Justice Curran. Just then there was a cry. Desmond Curran had found the dead body of his sister. Rutherford and Patricia's father ran to the scene and Rutherford's torch illuminated the sorry sight of the body. Rutherford bent down to examine it. He later reported that the blood on the body was crusted and congealed. The body was turned towards the left side with the right arm in the air.

Rutherford could see the stiffness of the body and that rigor mortis had set in for some time. There was no sign of all the things Patricia had been carrying with her when she boarded the bus.

Now a car pulled up on the drive next to where they were. It contained Malcolm Davidson, the Curran family solicitor and was driven by his wife. A number of questions now present themselves to us: where are Patricia's things, who phoned the solicitor and why and what is Mrs. Davidson doing there?

The RUC Constable noted that Mrs. Davidson clutched the wheel and did not even glance in the direction of the group in the drive way. Why not? Would you not have got out of the car out of prurient curiosity or shock or to say something ?

Now events took another bizarre turn and we have another set of questions emerging about this case.

The body with a Police Constable present was actually removed from the scene of the crime! Later when questioned by the police Desmond Curran alleged that he had lifted his sister's head and that he felt she was still breathing. Malcolm Davidson and Desmond Curran then lifted the body and manhandled it into Davidson's car. The body was so stiff that they have to lay it across their knees on the back seat and open the window so that the feet and legs stick through! Rutherford did not stop them. This was 1952 and deference to a man like Mr. Justice Lancelot Curran would be natural to a humble RUC constable. The car with its gruesome cargo then left and conveyed the body to the surgery of Dr. Wilson, the family doctor.

Now, it is worthwhile going back to the newspapers' description of the way in which the body had been laid out when Patricia was discovered. Patricia was turned towards her left side with her right arm straight up in the air. The problem here is gravity. On death a body goes limp. Patricia's right arm was stiffly in the air. Did she die where she was found? Did she die elsewhere where she fell onto her back with her arm out flung She then would have stiffened in that position. For all the stab wounds there was hardly any blood around the body. Had Patricia been murdered somewhere else and so had the body been placed where it was found?

Go back to Iain Hay Gordon's confession and he does say he dragged the body "through the bushes to hide it". Could this account for the state of the corpse? Her underwear was torn though she had not been assaulted and three buttons were eventually found some way from the body. It is worth noting that Hay Gordon was of slight build whereas Patricia was a big, athletic girl. Someone who knew them both said Patricia Curran could have pulled Hay Gordon through bushes but he was unlikely to have been able to do the same to her.

Now, where were the things Patricia had with her on the day she was murdered? No one reports seeing them anywhere about when the body had been discovered on the fateful night yet the press noted that there they were the next day sitting beside the driveway not far from where the body had been. There were her books, folder and handbag. Her shoes were sitting neatly side by side. Murdered and murderer appear to have been very daintily tidy. Was this dreadful murder as later alleged the result of a secret assignation gone horribly wrong? Still missing were the Squash racquet and her umbrella and the yellow Juliet cap she had been wearing on her head?

Those speculating that a cover up of some kind had taken place believe that if Patricia had been murdered elsewhere and if the body had been placed, then the crime scene the next day when the police examined it was a stage set.

Now for the biggest problem of all – the police investigation.

Two eye witnesses had seen Patricia Curran leave the bus at 5.50pm. The investigation had centered on the gap between that time and the time the body was found. The officer in charge of the case was Inspector McConnell of the RUC. McConnell from the start was hampered because he was under strict instructions from Sir Richard Pim, Inspector General of the RUC, that he was neither to question the Currans nor to enter the house. Were the wheels within wheels of a cover up conspiracy working? The investigation as followed by the press lists people the police wanted to question - a man seen in a

Carrickfergus café with hayseed in his hair, Polish servicemen, a man with a scarred face, a driver of an Austin 10 car, two women seen in the area. The impression is of an investigation confused and floundering. Pim then took the investigation out of the hands of the RUC and brought in two Scotland Yard heavies Inspector Capstick, known for brutal interrogation methods and his Detective-Sergeant, Hawkins. It is they who secure the arrest and confession of Iain Hay Gordon.

I leave you to consider these questions about the Curran case and like many readers of the Belfast dailies of 1952 to make up your own mind about the problems posed by the apparent facts:

1. Did Hay Gordon do it? He was an outsider, a loner, not the sharpest tack in the box. Painfully shy, he was picked up by Desmond Curran and invited to The Glen on several occasions so that Desmond Curran a devotee of Moral Rearmament could save his soul. Gordon had no alibi for the time of the murder and had asked another RAF man to lie for him. At the time he fitted the bill for a loner who might in a moment of insanity have lain in wait for Patricia Curran and brutally killed her.

2. If he did not do it then who did? Is this a motiveless killing or did someone have cause to kill Patricia?

3. What happened in the missing time between Patricia getting off the bus and when her body was found?

Those who want to look beyond Hay Gordon, a jilted lover or a random attacker ask whether she in fact did reach home? The RUC had been instructed not to search the house or question the Currans. If the RUC had been able to search the house would they have found the missing Squash racquet and umbrella there? Would Patricia's Juliet cap have been sitting on her dressing table? Had a terrible argument taken place in that house which resulted in someone losing control and Patricia being subjected to a frenzied attack?

Judge Curran usually spent his evenings at the Reform Club in the centre of Belfast. On the evening of the murder he was called to the phone at seven p.m. Eyewitnesses said he appeared agitated and hastily left. Why? What was in the

IAIN HAY GORDON

phone call to have so disturbed him?

Lastly, in 1956 The Glen was sold by the Currans. In 1959 the people who bought it decided to redecorate the house. They lifted a carpet in one of the bedrooms to reveal a large dark stain on the wooden floor boards. To them it looked like blood and so they informed the police. The RUC inspected the stain and told them not to worry it could have been caused by anything.

This is one of Northern Ireland's great unsolved murders; one about which many theories abound. What do you think?

January 1953

Two disasters bracket this month. On 5th January a Viking Class Airliner crashed at Aldergrove and on 31st of the same month the car ferry "Princess Victoria" sank. Both disasters resulted in great loss of life and shocked the whole province.

The Nutt's Corner Air Disaster 5th January 1953

January 1953 was the coldest January since the severely cold winter of 1945. Snow and gales which had begun in late December 1952 swept the British Isles. On the bitterly cold evening of 5th January a BEA Viking Class Airliner carrying thirty passengers and four crew was delayed from leaving on its routine flight from Northolt to Belfast by a technical fault. The passengers were Ulster people and included one infant. The fault was quickly fixed and the flight took off only slightly late.

At approximately 9.30pm the aircraft made its approach to Nutt's Corner Airfield. The weather on that evening was quite good with a cloud base of 1300 ft. The aircraft came in very low on its approach to the main runway and catastrophically struck a beacon and then a radio control building before crashing in a field 100yds from the runway. Wreckage was cast over a wide distance with one engine torn off and tossed into an adjoining field.

The scene which met the rescuers was horrific. One survivor, a young girl, was stopped as she was running hysterically down the runway away from the wreck: bodies were strewn around - some half in and half out of the wreckage. People had died from multiple injuries and shock. Survivors requiring urgent medical attention were quickly ferried to the Royal Victoria Hospital and to Antrim Hospital.

As can be seen from the1950s adverts for holidays and the proposal for a second airport at Sydenham air travel was becoming a popular option for the people of Northern Ireland so, an inquiry into the cause of this disaster was vital.

Had it been caused by a reoccurrence of the technical fault, the weather or human error?

The report of the inquiry was published in "The Belfast Newsletter" during the first week of February 1953. No pre-crash technical failure had been found. The plane was judged air worthy. Attention then turned to the conditions for the landing. There had been heavy rain that night and that had presented difficulties. The aircraft had been piloted that night by Captain Hartley, a pilot with over 20 years experience who had made 35 safe landings at Nutt's Corner.

He had opted for a ground controlled landing but because of poor visibility the Ground Controller advised Captain Hartley that he could not assist him. Hartley then told the Controller that the runway was visible and he would attempt a landing.

Survivors gave evidence that there was no problem as the plane made its approach – it was just a bit bumpy. However, one passenger who was seated in the 5th row from the back, Kathleen Brown a young QUB medical student, said she thought the plane was coming in too fast and too low. She saw orange coloured lights flashing past the window then the emergency door behind her burst open.

The aircraft had hit a radio beacon at the threshold of the runway.

The wounded plane managed a touchdown but then took off again. It skimmed the runway and crashed into a brick building which housed radio equipment. One can only imagine the struggle on board to control that plane but Captain Hartley had misjudged and paid a heavy price. The inquiry could only come to one conclusion. The verdict as to the cause of this tragic disaster was sadly, pilot error.

Sadly, there was to be a second air disaster at Nutt's Corner in October 1957 when a BEA Viscount crashed again in poor weather killing seven people on board including both pilots and three other crew. Eyewitnesses at the enquiry into this disaster said the plane seemed to be coming in to land when the pilot had aborted the landing and overshot the runway. Then there had been an explosion and the plane eventually had come to rest on marshy ground beyond the airfield. Wreckage had been strewn over a wide area. No one could explain why the landing had gone so terribly wrong.

The Princess Victoria Disaster. 31st January 1953

A cold morning on a County Down beach ; among the washed ashore Jellyfish the body of a woman. Bloated and nearly unrecognisable it had been in the sea for some time. The body was not that of a recent murder. It was all that remained of a poor victim of the sinking some weeks before of the Larne/Stranraer passenger ferry the "Princess Victoria".

The short sea crossing between Ulster and the West coast of Scotland is a familiar one to many. It can be as flat as a mill pond or as rough as going around Cape Horn. Nowadays crossings are cancelled in very high winds and rough seas and every precaution taken for passenger safety and comfort.

The crossing from Stranraer to Larne attempted by the "Princess Victoria on the morning of 31st January 1953 was to be a horrendous experience for all concerned and a fatal one for many.

The ship captained by Captain Ferguson was a six year old purpose built car ferry capable of taking 1,500 passengers and crew plus cargo.

On the morning of the 31st there was a crew of 49 and only 127 passengers. The crew consisted of men from both Larne and Stranraer. The Captain, First Officer and Radio Officer were all Stranraer men.

On the passenger list were a mixture of soldiers on leave, young mothers travelling alone with children and 23 Harland and Wolf men who were working at the yard in Scotland and on their way home for the weekend.

Also on board were Major J.M. Sinclair the MP for Belfast Cromac and Deputy Prime Minister of Northern Ireland and another M.P. Sir Walter Smiles, M.P. for North Down.

The weather was atrocious and worsening. No cars could be loaded because the high winds of 75 mph gusting to 80mph rendered inoperable the harbour cranes used to hoist them on board. The

THE ILL-FATED PRINCESS VICTORIA.

morning squalls of sleet and snow reduced visibility. Many thought the ship should never have even attempted to leave Stranraer. But Captain Ferguson, a very experienced seaman, took the "Princess Victoria " out. She left her dock 45 minutes late and set out into Loch Ryan.

Those who use this crossing know that in bad weather the loch at first gives a little shelter but that it does not take long on a rough crossing for the ship to begin to pitch and toss. The 176 souls on board knew the crossing would be bad but nothing could have prepared them for the terrifying conditions in the loch or the ferocity of the open sea. It is hard to imagine the horrors the passengers must have felt shut below in the claustrophobic saloon space as the sea crashed around the ferry and the ship began to roll up and down and side to side. People must have felt violently sea sick and very frightened.

Then as now ships leaving Loch Ryan round the Mull of Galloway as close to the Corsewall Point Light House as possible. By 8.30 am The Princess Victoria was clearing Corswall Point. Ahead was a gigantic sea. Captain Ferguson taking account of the difficulties facing him now decided to proceed no further and to turn the ship about and run before the storm back to Stranraer.

Disastrously this manoeuvre exposed the vulnerable rear doors of the ferry to the waves. Gigantic waves pounded against the doors which were only 5 foot high and would prove no bulwark against such force The doors eventually buckled. Water poured into the car deck. The Second Officer and 4 crew braved the elements to try to make safe the doors. Struggle as they might the breached doors could not be secured.

The captain now attempted to free the bow rudder to allow the ship to reverse towards Stranraer. Two sailors and the ship's carpenter were ordered forward to try this. But it was hopeless the bow rudder could not be freed; the release pin was immoveable. This is the fateful point when the cargo shifted and the ship alarmingly rolled to Starboard. Survivors said they now became aware of a distinct list.

Ferguson and his crew were making superhuman efforts to save the ferry but they were facing a near calamitous situation. The captain could not reverse to the safety of Loch Ryan. The buckled doors could completely give way at any moment if exposed further to the relentlessly battering waves.

There was only one throw of the dice left. The "Princess Victoria " had to call for assistance, keep her head into the wind and make for Larne

9.46am as gallons of water flooded the car deck an urgent message was sent from the stricken vessel to Portpatrick "Hove to off mouth of Loch Ryan. Vessel not under command. Urgent assistance of tug required."

By 10.31am all the passengers and crew were ordered to don their lifejackets. The list had become more marked. Next the crew tried to uncover the lifeboats. The increasing list hampered greatly this effort.

Only the survivors of the disaster can recount with accuracy the horrors of what followed.

For the rest of us the radio signals and our imagination will have to suffice to try to empathetically piece together the events of the next few hours. The brave radio operator was David Broadfoot. He was not one of those saved.

This is the gist of the messages he sent right to the last moments of the ship.

    12.52.   The starboard engine room was flooded.

    13.08   The ship was on her beam and the order to abandon ship had been given

    13.35   They could see the Irish coast

    13.47   They could see the Copelands lighthouse

    13.58   Broadfoot sent an S.O.S and the estimated position of the ship which was 5 miles east of the Copelands, virtually at the mouth of Belfast Lough and within grasp of safety.

At round about 2pm with only very few passengers in lifeboats the "Princess Victoria" slowly rolled over on to her hull. Lifeboat No.4. full of women and children was then hit by a huge wave, lifted up and dashed against the upturned ship. As the

sea receded nothing was left of the lifeboat or her passengers. Panicked passengers ran along the hull and in desperation decided to take their chances in the waves roaring around them as high as 40 feet. Their aim was to reach what lifeboats or life rafts there were or cling to the flotsam. But only the fittest could beat that sea and haul themselves on to the rafts. Lifeboat No.6 became packed. Young fit men were the ones who made it through and survived.

Where were the rescuers the ship had called for all day? They were searching but, in the wrong place. The lifeboats from Donaghadee and Portpatrick, three coasters, a trawler and H.M.S. Contest were 5 miles south of the last position given by the ship and were 50 minutes away. Fatally, "The Princess Victoria" in her last message had given a wrong estimate of her position

When the rescuers did arrive the weather had deteriorated to such an extent that they could not even begin to haul in the lifeboats and life rafts. The Donaghadee Lifeboat crew of the Sir Samuel Kelly could only watch helplessly as massive waves swept survivors off life rafts and as bodies in lifejackets were carried away. The coxswain, Hugh Nelson and his crew risked everything to pick up 34 people out of the water. H.M.S. Contest and the Portpatrick lifeboat plucked a further 9 survivors from the sea and one more was brought in by the trawler "Eastcoasts". No sooner had the Sir Samuel Kelly put in to port than she was off searching again. But no one else was found alive. Only empty life rafts and bodies. Of the 176 who left Stranraer on the morning of 31st January only 44 made it to safety. Captain, Officers, crew and the two prominent M.Ps were among those who died. All the women and children were lost.

Gradually the sea gave up the dead. Bodies were washed ashore along the Co.Down coast; two were found in a lifeboat at Kearney Point.

The bodies of 42 souls were never found. Deep sadness was felt both in Ulster and on the west coast of Scotland and expressed in memorial services on both sides of the Irish Sea.

A disaster fund was set up to help the survivors and the efforts of the Donaghadee crew and its valiant coxswain have passed into legend.

What part did the decisions and actions of the crew of the "Princess Victoria" contribute to this tragedy? Like the air disaster had a captain made a fatal error?

In June 1953 the inquiry into the disaster concluded that the vessel had been overwhelmed by weather and unforeseeable circumstances. It also judged that the ship was unseaworthy since the owners had not provided strong enough stern doors. The doors had been damaged in 1951 and the inquiry said the owners should have known that "sooner or later seas would be encountered which would subject those doors to severe trial". The second contributing factor was identified as the scuppers and the problem of releasing water through the ship. The court found the owners responsible for the loss. Ferguson may be thought unwise to have taken the vessel out but no one could doubt his efforts or that of his officers and crew in trying to save her.

To say that 1953 had got off to an inauspicious start would be an understatement. The Nutt's Corner Air Disaster had been followed by the "Princess Victoria" disaster. But they were followed in turn by even more ruin caused by appalling weather. In February high winds and torrential rain led to flooding in Belfast and to 285 known deaths in floods in England with 250,000 acres of land on England's east coast being flooded. So bad was the weather that even the dykes in Holland were breached and 1/6th of the country became water logged leaving one thousand Dutch dead and one million in distress. All this before anyone could blame extreme weather events on global warming.

CHAPTER 15

A BIT OF SPORT
"WE'RE NOT BRAZIL, WE'RE
NORTHERN IRELAND!"

For such a small place Northern Ireland has produced a lot of sporting champions. In the 1950s those with an interest in sport were spoilt for choice. The pages of the local newspapers were crammed with reports on sport of all kinds – football, cricket, hockey G.A.A., netball, boxing and so on. Sport even had its own paper – "Ireland's Saturday Night". When I started to look at this aspect of life in the 1950s I felt a comprehensive coverage within the scope of this book would be impossible; something would get short changed or overlooked. So, I am turning the spotlight only on events on the world stage – the Olympics 1956 and the World Cup 1958 – and on two outstanding Belfast sportspeople of the 1950s.

The Olympic Games of 1956 were nick-named the "Friendly Games" in contrast to the tension generated by world events at the time. In November of that year the USSR had invaded Hungary and ruthlessly crushed an uprising against USSR communist control of the country. The summer games of the XVIth Olympiad began in Melbourne three weeks later and in protest against the participation of the USSR Holland and Spain refused to send competitors.

At the previous games held in Helsinki in 1952 Great Britain had won only one Gold Medal; it was in the show-jumping. In the Melbourne games hopes were pinned on Belfast girl Thelma Hopkins to win a Gold in athletics. In May, 1956 Thelma Hopkins had already set a new World record of 5ft 8 ½ ins in the High-jump at Cherryvalley Playing Fields in east Belfast. A plaque at Cherryvalley now marks that occasion. Thelma was not only competing in the High-jump

but also was going for the double with a bid to also win a Gold in the Long-jump. The glory of the double was not to be. Thelma injured her ankle in training and on the day of the long-jump competition [27th November] competed with the ankle heavily bandaged. She failed to qualify for the final.

In the High-jump the Gold also eluded her. She tied for the Silver with the Russian, Pirsareva - both jumped 5ft 5 ¾ ins. The Gold and plus Thelma's World Record were claimed by the American high-jumper, McDaniels with a winning jump of 5ft 9 ¾ ins.

Thelma Hopkins was an outstanding all-rounder – she returned to Belfast from the Olympics and immediately turned out for Senior Ulster Women's Hockey trials. Needless to say she got her place on the team.

Thelma was not the only competitor from Belfast to appear in the Melbourne Olympics and return with a medal. Two Boxers, Freddy Gilroy and John Caldwell, turned out for the Republic of Ireland team. Gilroy was outpointed in his Bantamweight semi-final and Caldwell, a flyweight, lost to a Romanian in his semi-final. Both Belfast men ended up with creditable Bronze medals.

One big story from the games was the Hungary versus USSR Waterpolo game – a needle match if ever there was one. It nearly ended in an all out fist fight. In a competitively fought moment one Hungarian player sustained an injury and, blood pouring from a head wound, had to leave the pool. Hungarian supporters then stormed the poolside accusing the Russians of starting a rough-house.

Officials had a wild job trying to calm everybody down. However, the whole incident seems to have put fire in the bellies of the Hungarian team as it went on to hammer the USSR 4- 0.

Back home in Hungary on 9th December the USSR military declared the country was under martial law. At the end of the Olympics 56 out of the 113 Hungarian competitors decided to defect and approached the Australian authorities about staying put in Australia.

Rugby matches between the home nations attracted huge crowds in the 1950s. In 1957 Ireland played Wales in a Rugby International at Cardiff Arms Park. Wales beat the Irish by two penalties to one. It was a match played in conditions so atrocious that the referee had to order the Welsh to change into fresh jerseys so that he could distinguish between the two sides. Ireland took the lead in the match when JR Kavanagh went over the line and scored Ireland's only penalty of the game. A team – mate then rushed over and enthusiastically hugged him – a sight not unfamiliar in the modern game but not so common in the 1950s. The hug prompted an outraged response from one spectator, "This sort of adulation has no place on a Rugby field."

But, if anyone deserved that sort of adulation it surely had to be the Rugby hero of the 1950s Belfast man Jack Kyle. He had a distinguished career winning 46 caps for Ireland between 1947 and 1958 as a wily fly-half. He also gained six caps in 1950 when playing for the British and Irish Lions on their tour of New Zealand and Australia. Jack Kyle is still a Rugby legend in Northern Ireland.

1958 was a Football World Cup year. The competition was held from 8-29th June in Sweden and in a never to be repeated situation all four home nations qualified. Northern Ireland had qualified at the expense of Italy! In another first the World Cup was to be televised across Western Europe.

England's hopes of doing well in the competition had been dealt a bitter blow by the loss of so many Manchester United players, including the England Captain, Duncan Edwards, in the Munich Air Disaster which had happened in February. A Northern Irish player, Jackie Blanchflower, was ruled out of the Northern Ireland World Cup team because he had sustained a broken pelvis, breaks to his ribs and arm plus internal injuries. A Republic of Ireland player, Billy Whelan, had also been killed in the crash. The Northern Ireland goalkeeper, Harry Gregg who played brilliantly throughout the World Cup tournament was a survivor of the crash.

In the draw Northern Ireland managed by Peter Doherty was drawn in Group One with a group of teams calculated to make any modern team manager's heart hit his boots – West Germany, Czechoslovakia and Argentina. The Scots were up against France, Paraguay and Yugoslavia. The Welsh faced Mexico, Hungary and the home nation, Sweden and England was drawn against Russia, Austria and Brazil. Debuting for Brazil was a footballing legend in the making, the seventeen year old Pele.

Concern had been expressed by sabbatarians in Northern Ireland that the Northern Ireland team would have to play some of their matches on Sundays; as fate would have it Northern Ireland ended up scheduled to play two Sunday games.

On 8th June the team played the Czechs. Northern Ireland took the lead in the fifteenth minute with a brilliant goal from Wilbur Cush and desperate defending by Harry Gregg in goal kept the team in the lead to the bitter end.

On Wednesday 15th N. Ireland defeated Argentina 3-1. Now all N.Ireland had to do was to beat the current World Cup holders West Germany to advance to the quarter- finals! The match would be played on 15th June – a Sunday! To compound the offence given to the sabbatarians at home the Governor of Northern Ireland, Lord Wakehurst, stated that he intended to be a spectator.

In an exciting match in which the goalkeeper, Gregg brought off several brilliant saves Northern Ireland nearly succeeded in pulling off one of the biggest shocks of the tournament. The two teams were 2-2 when, with just seven minutes to go in the match, McParland broke through the West German defence and fired off a header towards the goal. It hit the crossbar. W.Germany thoroughly rattled then resorted to time wasting – one free kick took a whole minute.

At this stage in Group 1 W. Germany had four points, Northern Ireland and Czechoslovakia had three and the Argentineans two. There would have to be a play off between the Ulster men and the Czechs to determine which side went through to the Quarters.

Tuesday 17th, Malmo – N. Ireland progressed to the quarter-finals of the World Cup by beating Czechoslovakia 2-1. This was a hard fought contest. With the score standing at 1-1 it went to 15 minutes of extra time. After seven minutes of the extra time, with darkness falling, Cush took a free kick which connected with Blanchflower who chipped it on to an unmarked McParland. He slammed it right footed into the Czech goal! Play grew rough and desperate in the final three minutes. A Czech was sent off for a terrible tackle on Cunningham and when the final whistle blew the pitch was littered with injured and exhausted players.

It was a victory for the N. Ireland men but a bit of a Pyrrhic one. The team had too many star players injured to give a good account of themselves in its quarter-final match against France and hopes of a place in the semi-finals were dashed by a 4-0 defeat. Since then supporters have speculated what might have happened if only the team had had more than one day's rest after that Czech game. If the team had beaten France only Brazil and Pele in the semi stood between N. Ireland and the World Cup Final!

CHAPTER 16

CHICKEN BOY, MAURA AND THE EVANGELICALS AND FETHARDISM

IN SEPTEMBER AND OCTOBER of 1956 people throughout Northern Ireland were shocked by the distressing stories in the newspapers of the case of a small boy found in a hen house in Co. Down. The newspapers had quickly named the child, "Chicken Boy".

The sad story came to light in September when four boys playing near a henhouse heard strange noises coming from within and what they thought was someone crying. They tried the door. It was locked. Then one boy, more venturesome than the others, looked through the window. Two eyes looked back at him. Was it a dog? Gradually, as his eyes became accustomed to the gloomy interior, the boy made out the figure of a small, filthy, naked boy. Another noise this time from the house – the occupant, Mrs. Halfpenny had returned from work. The startled children scarpered and alerted adults. The police and NSPCC were subsequently called.

The boy from the chicken house judged to be between six and seven years old was Kevin Halfpenny. He was taken to Nazareth Lodge a Children's Home in Belfast and the child's condition was assessed. Kevin was pale and thin weighing only two stone fully clothed. He was just two foot six inches tall and could not stand unaided. Kevin was pronounced "retarded but not mentally deficient". His misshapen arm and leg joints were consistent with having had rickets a disease which is caused by a lack of vitamin D the main source of which is sunlight It generally appears in children at about nine months of age so Kevin at six or seven years old had been an untreated victim for up to five years. Years spent in the darkness and filth of that henhouse?

The conditions the child had been confined in were atrocious. Investigators found half an inch depth of animal filth and excrement on the floor of the henhouse together with human hair. There was an overpowering, nauseating smell of urine.

In October Kevin's mother was taken to court on charges of neglect and wilful mistreatment. She defended her actions by saying that when he was younger she had tried to teach Kevin to walk and talk but he could do neither. She had to go out to work and he could not be left alone so she had locked him up for his own safety. Mrs. Halfpenny maintained that Kevin was fed and was never locked out in the winter. It was also stated in her defence that she had been widowed at a young age and left with only a poor farm to let out. Her defence pointed out that Mrs. Halfpenny had brought up her other four children and had reared them well.

In November the case came to a conclusion and Mrs. Halfpenny was sentenced to nine months for wilful neglect of Kevin.

There is an awful sadness in this case. Kevin was an illegitimate child: to 1950s thinking, a shameful being who had to be shut away from the disapproval of society. This morally uptight society's disapprobrium rained down on unmarried mothers who were often encouraged to give their babies away to strangers for adoption. The attitude towards illegitimacy allowed back street abortionists to thrive and ply their dangerous trade. The heartache caused must have been terrible to bear.

In October 1956 as the Halfpenny case reached its conclusion a small item of news appeared in the Belfast newspapers. It concerned another minor.

Maura Margaret Lyons a fifteen and a half year old factory worker of 78 Iris Drive, Falls Road, Belfast was reported as missing. If anything the case of Maura Lyons was to prove even more sensational than that of the Chicken Boy.

Maura and The Evangelicals

To fully grasp the sensation caused by the disappearance and reappearance of Maura Lyons as a "born again" evangelical one has to briefly explore the emergence in 1950s Belfast of fire brand evangelical

Protestantism. Spear heading this movement was the Evangelical Protestant Society with Norman Porter as Secretary and Ian Paisley as Treasurer. This group saw itself called to lead a crusade against what it called "Popery". "Popery" it defined as an amalgam of a "Romeward trend" plus a push towards the secularisation of society. Thus any clergy attempting to discuss Christian unity were denigrated as "ecumaniacs" and any effort to unchain swings in the public parks on Sundays was seen as the road to Hell! Evangelical Protestants classified themselves as "Bible Christians" and "God's own people". The group most vehement in its evangelical Protestantism was Ian Paisley's newly arrived Free Presbyterian Church. Free Presbyterians were loud and zealous in defence of what they held to be true and right. They were also energetically proselytising; preaching at street corners and holding prayer meetings in work places.

On the 15th November 1956 the "Belfast Newsletter" reported that Mr. Harry Diamond [Republican Labour, Falls] had stated in the Stormont House of Commons that Maura Lyons a Roman Catholic girl from the Falls had been taken from her home by a Free Presbyterian minister, Rev. David Leathem. Diamond implied this Roman Catholic girl had been kidnapped by evangelical Protestants.

December unfolded with bitter accusations that the girl was being held against her will and there were heated exchanges between unionists and nationalists in Stormont on the matter. Meanwhile the RUC investigation in to Maura's disappearance took D.I. MacMillan to England to follow up leads. Then, sensationally on 20th December at an evangelical Free Presbyterian rally in the Ulster Hall a tape recording was played of what was alleged to be Maura Lyons telling of her conversion from Roman Catholicism. The next thing that happened was very strange.

After six months, on 10th May 1957, when the RUC investigation had drawn a blank Maura turned up on the doorstep of 423 Beersbridge Road, Belfast, the home of Rev. Ian Paisley. She said who she was and told Mrs. Paisley to contact the Police. The first thing Mrs. Paisley did was to put the tea pot on. It was Rev. Ian Paisley who phoned the police at Ballyhackamore. Maura was then taken to Templemore Avenue RUC Station and there the story of her disappearance was told.

Maura said she had been converted to Protestantism by friends at work and that when she had told her parents her father had flown into a rage and struck her.

This her father later denied. Maura then said that when she returned from work the next night there were three priests in the house and that she thought she was going to be taken away to a convent. She had then packed a bag and sneaked out of the family home.

There was undoubtedly involvement by others in whisking Maura out of the country and sheltering her for the six months prior to her return. But in the end no person was held to account for the disappearance of this underage girl.

On Sunday 12 May Paisley claimed Maura Lyons as a convert not to Free Presbyterianism but to Christianity. He said she had wanted to come to his church that Sunday but was being held in a Welfare Home. On the 16th the girl was made a Ward of Court. Maura later reconverted to Roman Catholicism.

Harry Diamond alleged there was a conspiracy by evangelical Protestants to abduct and brainwash people. He based his belief on the fact that Maura was not the only one who had disappeared. Another girl, Kathleen Kelly this time from a Church of Ireland background had left her home in Benburb Street. A letter from this girl who was 18 years old and therefore not underage then appeared in the "Belfast Newsletter" stating that she was exercising her civil and religious rights. Miss Kelly maintained she was not forced to do anything against her will and that her only influence was "the word of God in which I wholeheartedly believe and which is fearlessly preached in the Free Presbyterian Church in Ulster."

These at the time sensational cases gifted Paisley's church and right wing Protestantism the oxygen of publicity which was to encourage its growth and development in the '50s and '60s into a political as well as a religious movement. Their cause was then given another unexpected and further boost.

Fethardism

The suspicions of the Free Presbyterians that all Protestants on the island of Ireland were the victims of a Roman Catholic plot to do them down appeared to be justified when in May 1957 the Belfast newspapers began to carry the story of the apparent victimisation of Protestants in the Co. Wexford village of Fethard – on –Sea. The relations between Roman Catholics and Protestants [largely Church of Ireland] in the village had been good until a local woman Mrs. Sheila Clooney, a Protestant, had left her husband [a Roman Catholic farmer] taking their two young daughters with her. Mrs. Clooney had left her home on the morning of 27th April. What provoked Mrs. Clooney into fleeing from the family farm was the prospect of having to start her eldest daughter, Eileen Mary, at the local Roman Catholic Primary school on the 29th April.

What followed was to turn into a national disgrace for the Republic of Ireland and to play out sensationally in the Belfast newspapers.

The local parish priest accused the small Protestant community of the village of aiding and abetting Mrs. Clooney's flight, condemned Sheila Clooney's actions and urged his parishioners to boycott all Protestant businesses in the village. This greatly affected two Protestant shops Cooper's and Gardiner's and other Protestants in the village such as the music teacher and even the milkman There was a single-teacher Protestant Primary in the village and the teacher appointed was a Roman Catholic. She was "persuaded" to give up her post thus closing the eleven pupil school.

In the North right-wing Protestant clerical and political outrage knew no bounds. They claimed everything they had said would happen to Protestants in a Roman Catholic dominated Irish state was justified - "Home Rule was Rome Rule".

However political reaction in the South was not totally in favour of the Fethard boycott. De Valera through a spokesman described the boycott as "futile" and urged that it should stop. In the Republic's Senate Dr. Owen Sheehy Skeffington said the Republic's people were shamed by the events at Fethard. He was particularly concerned that the Protestant children of the village had been deprived of their education by the forced resignation of their teacher. In contrast the Leader of the House dismissed the issue saying it was just a purely local matter.

In the Republic a real State / Church split then emerged. The government of the South was fully conscious of the matter being seen as one of how the Protestant minority was treated. It also had the worry that the issue was being played out against the background of a violent IRA border campaign in the North. Therefore there was pressure for the Republic to be seen as a responsible, friendly neighbouring power.

However the Irish Roman Catholic hierarchy failed to help in resolving the situation and if anything made it worse. The Bishop of Wexford in whose diocese the boycott was occurring issued a statement in which he described the boycott as, "a moderate and peaceful protest" and accused the Press of creating a bad atmosphere by exaggerating what the local Roman Catholics of Fethard were doing. The Bishop of Galway added his tuppence worth in support of the boycotters saying it was just a little local incident. Then, in a sermon at a Sunday mass, the parish priest of Fethard positively encouraged the boycott by stating,

"The priests of this parish with a full sense of their responsibility and realising the Catholic issue at stake assure the faithful, loyal Catholics of this parish that in the stand they are taking in defence of Catholic principles, not now, nor in the near future, will their priests let them down by asking them to withdraw one inch or apologise for their actions." The priest also stated that the boycott had the backing not only of their Bishop but also of the Roman Catholic Primate himself, Cardinal d'Alton!

De Valera was placed in a real predicament by these unhelpful clerics. The whole question of the position of the Protestant minority in the South had been highlighted by this issue. Were Protestants full citizens of the Republic or barely tolerated resident aliens? Could the South protest about the treatment of the Roman Catholic minority in the North if its own house was not in order? Protests from northern and southern Protestants were coming thick and fast as in August the boycott rolled into its fourth month. A prominent group of Roman Catholic laity in the North was prompted to draft an open letter which was published in the Belfast newspapers stating that they wished to disassociate themselves from the action taken and that the boycott must be deplored "by all right-thinking people".

A masterstroke of realpolitik was called for. In a move against the IRA perpetrators of the border campaign de Valera recovered the government's position and earned the praise of unionists by introducing internment in the South and rounding up 63 IRA suspects.

While all this was on-going where was Mrs. Clooney?

Wind back the clock to the first week in May. At the Belfast High Court a writ of Habeas Corpus had been granted against Mrs. Clooney and Mr Desmond Boal. The writ demanded that they produce the Clooney children. How was Boal, a Belfast barrister involved in this case? Boal was aligned to the right wing Protestant cause.

He had turned up at the Clooney farm on 30th April, the day after Mrs. Clooney's disappearance with a list of demands to be met if she was to return home. Mrs. Clooney wanted the family farm to be sold and the family to emigrate to Canada or Australia.

The crunch demand was that her husband had to convert to Protestantism. Mr. Clooney refused to meet any of the conditions and demanded to know where his wife and children were. He then came to Belfast in search of his family.

Suspicion for the disappearance of Mrs. Clooney and her daughters again fell on supporters of the Rev. Ian Paisley. She and the two little girls appeared to have been spirited away to Scotland and then to one of the centres of "wee Free" Presbyterianism – the Orkney Islands.

The eventual outcome was reconciliation between husband and wife and an end to the notorious boycott. The Clooney's returned to their farm and agreed that the girls would be home-schooled. However the word "Fethardism" -"to practise boycott along religious lines"-had now entered the English language

The question remains – would this domestic dispute have grown so disastrously out of hand if it had not been for the attitude of the Roman Catholic clergy and the interference of the evangelical Protestant Free Presbyterians? The seriousness with which it was treated shows it to be another sad reflection of the times. It mixes in with the fears of northern Protestants about their fate if they ever ended up in an un-partitioned Ireland and justified their determination to not "give an inch" on any issue they saw as threatening the status quo in Ulster. Thus the politics of Northern Ireland, with a big or small "P", nurtured on those fears was always vigilant in keeping the minority firmly into its place and condemning the perceived theocracy of the southern state.

CHAPTER 17

A LAST GLANCE AT 1950s POLITICS

A WHOLE BOOK COULD be devoted to this topic alone. Intentionally my approach will not be in-depth but that of the broad brush in looking at relations between North and South, the workings of Stormont and those of the predecessor of the present Belfast City Council, the Belfast Corporation. There are some things going on in politics in the 1950s which no-one could make up. There is a level of immature bickering which is breathtaking and not too many shining moments. Sadly, some would say that things have not changed much.

There is no doubt that the 1950s were the sunny uplands for the Ulster Unionists. de Valera's 1937 Constitution for Eire claimed jurisdiction over the whole island. However the departure of the Republic of Ireland from the Commonwealth in 1949 had prodded the British into issuing "The Guarantee" to the Ulster Unionists that Northern Ireland could not be forced into an all-Ireland situation without the consent of the Stormont Government which the unionists of course dominated. With this firmly tucked under their belt the unionists could count on the absentee landlordism of Westminster and cock a snoot at both the Republic and the nationalist minority within Northern Ireland.

Unionists dominated by virtue of superiority of numbers but also by the device of not adopting the same voting procedure as that of the rest of Great Britain – one man: one vote. In Northern Ireland the requirement that voters must be rate-payers and the practice of multiple voting worked in unionist favour. Workers from the South were not allowed to flood into the North. This immigration was stymied by the requirement of work permits. In areas where nationalists might out vote unionists gerrymander was brought into play and electoral boundaries cleverly manipulated [as in nationalist wards in Londonderry] to produce unionist majorities.

In relation to their attitude to their neighbours on the island, both outside the northern state and within, the unionist population took its lead from the Northern Ireland Prime Minister, Lord Brookeborough. He was at the helm throughout the '50s.

The unionist hierarchy was littered with the descendants of the landed gentry but the Brookeboroughs were unionist aristocracy. Brookeborough like his predecessors and successors as leaders of the Ulster Unionist Party was also a member of the Orange Order.

Brookeborough exuded an air of triumphalism over his nationalist opponents and was guilty from time to time of making absolutely sectarian comments. Of course, such comments made by either side were perfectly acceptable in the "gloves off" atmosphere of the time. He was capable of blithely assuring an audience that in Ulster,"We are all Britishers" when obviously there were those whose allegiance lay elsewhere. He firmly believed that the achievement of parity in welfare, health and social services with Britain would naturally lead the minority to know on which side its bread was buttered and so give up any dreams of Irish unity.

But in an 1958 election broadcast on behalf of the Nationalist Party given almost ten years before the whole situation in Northern Ireland was blown apart, its leader Eddie McAteer made a prophetic statement which summed up the true feelings of that community:

"Grievous burdens are placed on us because we will not hand over our schools to the tender mercies of those who hate us so much. Electoral boundaries are rigged to preserve for a little longer the fiction that our people really don't exist. One tragic result is that our people have lost faith in democratic institutions. When everybody is busy calling the IRA names, remember that we have many times predicted that the frustration and cynicism of our political life would inevitably lead to violence."

At Stormont and in Belfast Corporation there was no effective opposition to unionist rule. Under the old election arrangements Queen's University was entitled to four seats at Stormont. The university voters elected four Liberals. This was totally untypical of the voting pattern in the province where voting was split along strongly sectarian lines. However, nationalists were split into small factional groups – the Anti-Partition League, Eire Labour, Republican Labour, the Nationalist Party and the abstentionist Sinn Fein. The Northern Ireland Labour Party which should have attracted more votes from the working class was hindered because of fears about its attitude to partition.

In contrast the Ulster Unionist Party representing the Protestant majority presented one strong, solid bloc. There were from time to time independent unionists like Tommy Henderson and Norman Porter but, in Parliament and Council Chamber, on any matter, all unionists could combine to push legislation through.

Since lack of opposition could rarely effect their outcome debates often degenerated into little more than one side sniping at the other. A good example of this sniping came during the debate at Stormont to introduce the 1951 Census when a Unionist suggested that people should be asked to state the religion of their employer –

"with this information it would be possible to refute the slanderous accusations of discrimination which are made against Northern Ireland."

Quick as a flash the Nationalist MP for NE Tyrone countered by saying that the Unionist MP would be surprised by the figures if local [i.e. Unionist] councils were asked to state the religion of all their employees. This prompted another Unionist to stick his tuppence worth in by asking how many Protestants were employed in Monaghan, Cavan and Donegal councils. The Finance Minister, Major Maynard Sinclair then topped off this enlightened exchange by adding yet more fuel to the fire by asserting that if the number of Protestants employed by Roman Catholics was looked at it would be nil!

Bickering was no less in Belfast Corporation's debating chamber where Unionists also dominated. In March 1953 the debate on the Council's plans to celebrate the Coronation led to one nationalist Councillor being slung out of the Chamber. The Councillor in question was Alderman McKearney [Eire Labour]. He had refused to leave after being handed a suspension for remarks he made a few days earlier concerning the Corporation's plans to decorate two Public Parks situated in nationalist areas - Falls and Dunville

You have to sympathise with the logic of Councillor McKearney's argument when he points out that for the last coronation [that of George Vlth] the oak which the Council had insisted was planted in Falls Park had been ripped out the next day.

The apparently ill-considered determination of the unionists to force pro-British decorations into a nationalist area is evidence of the points McAteer was making in his election speech.

When the Deputy Lord Mayor had Alderman McKearney escorted from the Chamber another nationalist Councillor obviously with a gift for the dramatic was heard to remark,

"This is another example of gunman dictatorship and the Gestapo."

Unionists could just shrug this sort of thing off. They believed that anyone not supporting the Crown had an option – they could go South. Why should the unionists accommodate another point of view. They did not have to. There was no smack on the wrist from the British government for any unreasonable unionist behaviour. Unionist loyalty to the Crown was regularly endorsed and rewarded by visits of members of the royal family.

In 1953, in spite of threats from the self- proclaimed IRA splinter group Saor Uladh [Free Ulster] the recently crowned Queen visited Belfast. So confident were the authorities of the inability of nationalists to disrupt this visit that the entire itinerary was published in the local press. It gave exact times and the routes the royal car would follow.

On Thursday 2nd July the Queen would be at Balmoral Showgrounds and then progress in the royal car from there along the Stranmillis Embankment to Queen's University. This route took her over the King's Bridge right outside our front door at 85, Sunnyside Bungalows. There were no police, no barricades, no protecting marksmen. Our family lined up at the edge of the pavement, cheered and waved our mini Union Jacks. Her Majesty graciously waved. She was so close we could have touched her.

On her arrival at Queen's she was welcomed by Brookeborough who said, "We are all Queen's men today......"

Well, not quite. Already sixteen members of the Ulster Senate had refused to sign the proclamation recognising the Queen's authority over Ulster. Posters had appeared – "England – we want our country – not your Queen." Nationalists had been outraged by the Irish

Ambassador actually attending a reception at Buckingham Palace and worse, shaking hands with the Queen.

Eventually Cardinal d'Alton in a diplomatic move sent a goodwill message but, with a jag in it –

"All of us who love the old historic Ireland sincerely hope that during it [the Queen's reign] we may see our country restored to its natural unity."

One obvious way in which political affiliation and disunity is shown in Belfast is by the marking of territory This is done by the flying of flags, bunting and the painting of curb stones. In recent years this has produced some strange things. A few years ago the flying of the Royal Standard seemed to indicate that the Queen had given Balmoral the go by and was spending her summer in the Braniel Estate. West Belfast appeared to be full of Palestinians and Israelis and if you went by the flags, the French had invaded Finaghy Road South.

In the 1950s Unionists had Orange Order arches, union flags, red, white and blue kerbstones and bunting and gable wall murals of "King Billy" on his white horse. Nationalist areas favoured bunting in the Papal colours of blue and yellow and the display of Irish tricolours. In 1954 the unionists tried to put a stop to such nationalist displays of loyalty to the Irish Republic by passing "The Flags and Emblems Display Bill". The union flag was to fly "without let or hindrance"; the flying of the Irish tricolour was to be forbidden. In the Assembly Halls of schools controlled by the Belfast Education Authority photographs of the Queen and the Duke of Edinburgh flanked by the Ulster and the Union flags were proudly displayed. Anyone trying to display an Irish tricolour could be charged with attempting to provoke a breach of the public peace.

Needless to say the debate at Stormont over the passing of this bill produced the usually high level of mature and rational debate! A nationalist member got himself suspended for guess what - waving a tricolour. A unionist who just happened to have a union flag in his pocket then produced it and started to wave it. In response another nationalist produced a tricolour and waved it and so on, tit for tat. It would be funny if it was not so sad.

However, in 1956, there was a rare example of unionist and nationalist cooperation to scupper a measure which would have seriously affected hundreds of people, nationalist and unionist, who rented their homes from private landlords. Some of these landlords were notorious for doing no repairs and allowing their tenants to live in very poorly maintained accommodation. With the demand for housing so high the government had to try to ensure the upkeep of the existing housing stock and so decided to pass a "Rents Bill" compelling landlords to do repairs before they could increase rents. Any tenant who felt the landlord was neglecting their house could take the landlord to court to demand repairs.

This sounds eminently sensible but the bill seriously worried tenants. On 21st March 1956, the day the Rents Bill came up for its second reading, representatives of tenants' associations converged on Stormont in protest. From their point of view a landlord could do a minimum repair and then put up the rent substantially. They believed the bill did not protect the tenant but was a landlords' charter. How could tenants afford to take a landlord to court?

MPs whose constituencies were in working class areas decided to oppose the bill either by abstaining from the vote or voting against. Ulster Unionists against the bill included the MPs for St Anne's, Oldpark, Pottinger, Woodvale, Carrick and Cromac. They joined forces with Porter, Independent Unionist [Clifton], Morgan, Eire Labour [Dock], Diamond, Republican Labour [Falls], Hanna Independent Labour [Belfast Central] and Connellan, Nationalist [South Down].

Warnock, MP for St Anne's, actually had the courage to speak out against his party leader in the debate saying the government had "taken up peashooters against the dragon [of bad housing] and loaded them with tenants' money." Through their cross party cooperation the opposing MPs forced significant amendments to the bill which ensured tenants got fairer treatment.

This rare example of representatives crossing the divide, working together for the good of all the people, can be offset by yet another example of something that may seem to us today as daftness but which was taken seriously at the time.

In 1955, Mr. Norman Porter, Independent Unionist for Clifton, an MP who took it upon himself to assiduously guard Ulster against takeover bids by the Irish Republic spotted an attempted encroachment in an unusual area – the employment of mannequins[models] from the

Irish Republic by some of Belfast's top shops. Shops such as Robinson and Cleaver's, Brand's and Norman's, Anderson and Macauley's regularly held fashion shows for their female customers. At these models paraded about in the latest wear.

An outraged Mr. Porter actually went as far as raising the matter in the Northern Ireland Parliament and demanding an assurance that all the girls so employed were good Ulster [one suspects this should read Protestant] girls. Mr Healey, Nationalist [South Fermanagh] to great laughter pointed out that many Ulster girls were employed as mannequins in the South and said he hoped there was " no objection to a reciprocity in good looks". Porter was not to be put off his stroke so easily. He produced corroborating evidence in the form of model agency owner Mrs. Norma Ward who verified for him that unemployment among models from Northern Ireland did exist while the big stores drafted in good-looking Southerners. His next step was to be photographed on the steps of Stormont with a bevy of very good looking though sadly unemployed Ulster models. Porter then invited them into the Strangers' Gallery of the Debating Chamber to see him take up cudgels on their behalf.

MANNEQUINS LOBBY M.P.s

Regrettably, the models and Mr. Porter failed to note two big fellows in belted raincoats also occupying the gallery. When the debate began these buckos rose up and shouted, "Up the Republic!". Enter the RUC and the republican supporters and the models were ignominiously turfed out.

The mighty threat of subversive mannequins from the Irish Republic was eventually seen off by the Minister of Labour assuring Porter that all such mannequins would require work permits before being employed in Ulster shops! Phew! Now maybe Stormont could get back to the more serious matters of poor housing and unemployment.

All this bickering and sniping between nationalists and unionists did little to address the economic woes of Northern Ireland and in particular, Belfast. Unemployment never fell below 5% and by 1958 over 9% of the working population had no work. To be fair, while the impression is given that MPs and Councillors preferred snarling at each other rather than combining their efforts to make life easier for the people the work of the Ministry of Commerce had created over 32,000 new jobs. But few were east of the Bann and they were not enough to take up the greater numbers left by the decline and closure of Belfast's traditional industries.

Maybe the lack of focus on "bread and butter" issues was the voters fault. In every kind of election it was not the issue of the economy but the question of Britishness and the border which determined the votes of most voters.

In the 1959 Westminster election Ulster Protestant Action sent letters containing these two questions to all unionist candidates:

Question 1 – Do you believe the Union Jack should fly everywhere in Northern Ireland and will you use your influence to see that it does?

Question 2 – If you are elected will you sponsor a motion for the proscribing of Sinn Fein in Great Britain as an illegal organisation?

S.A.E.s accompanied the letters. To the credit of the unionist candidates only one responded and he was under threat of Paisley standing against him.

Two women candidates for Westminster seats in this election did try to turn the voters' attention to other matters. Contesting West Belfast Patricia McLaughlin put an emphasis on jobs, pensions and better housing for all while Sheila Murnaghan's campaign in South Belfast emphasised the importance of social justice, tolerance and freedoms. McLaughlin as a unionist was elected whereas Murnaghan, a Liberal, was bashed down by the question of where she stood in relation to Partition and lost.

But, voting figures for the 1959 election show a change is coming in terms of unionist control of the city of Belfast. The population of voters was shifting. People had moved out of the city to new housing estates on the fringes or to new towns like Newtownabbey. All in all there was a loss of 15,279 voters. In the long term this would lead to a decrease in vital votes for unionists in some marginal constituencies like West Belfast.

No wonder then that in 1959 Patricia McLaughlin [Unionist] had stated her intention to get on her bike and canvass votes in her constituency – carefully avoiding the times of the most popular T.V. programmes. In fact, in spite of all her efforts, her majority in West Belfast was dramatically cut from 18141 [1955] to 8836 [1959].

Of course in 1955 when Mrs. McLaughlin had captured the West Belfast seat one wag had said that the whole of Shankill Road graveyard must have voted for her!

What of Belfast Corporation? In an election all of the councillors had to stand for re -election and elections were held for Aldermen as and when they retired. Unionists tended to contest all seats except staunchly nationalist ones like Falls and Smithfield. Other parties fought very strategic elections putting up candidates where they thought they had a chance.

The Corporation was a microcosm of the Stormont parliament except in one respect. The unionist party in the city ran several women as candidates in Corporation elections. In May 1958 nine women stood for election of which seven were Ulster Unionists and the others Northern Ireland Labour.

Six of the nine were standing for re-election. Two failed to get elected – Mrs. Armstrong [Unionist] for St. George's Ward and Miss McKeown [NILP] standing for Woodvale Ward. One successful candidate Mrs. Breakey [Ulster Unionist] went on to be appointed High Sherriff.

It was the job of the Corporation to administer the City in the 1950s era of austerity. There was not much money about and the major issues which had to be addressed such as job creation, slum clearance and house building, the provision of schools and the emerging problem of traffic congestion in the city centre required vast investment and innovative thinking.

One innovative scheme eventually put on the back-burner because of lack of finance was revealed in September 1958. This was the proposal to build a tunnel under the River Lagan to link up the North and South approaches to the city on the Antrim side with the East and West approaches on the Down side of the Lough. The proposed cost was a cool £9 million. It is interesting to compare what was proposed by the City Surveyor in 1958 with the present system of roads, flyovers and bridges.

The approach to the tunnel from the Antrim side was to be from York Street via an entrance at Nile Street. The tunnel would then run in a straight line under Clarendon Dock and the river. The traffic would cross below the East Approach Road at Foundry Street and emerge at Cuba Street. Traffic travelling in the opposite direction would enter a roundabout which had exits to the East Approach Road Newtownards Road [at Templemore Avenue] and Dee Street. This gave the driver the choice of opting for a route to the city centre, or one up the Newtownards Road or to cross to the Antrim side via the tunnel.

Of course houses would have to be demolished to make way for the scheme but the City Surveyor assured the Corporation that they had been ear marked for slum clearance anyway. When it took cold feet over the cost the Corporation was told the alternative was a motorway system which would cost a lot more. For lack of finance both schemes were mothballed.

Traffic congestion in the city centre also necessitated the remodelling of routes in and around Donegall Place. With regard to the new road system around the City Hall much debate was given over to the siting of the Titanic Memorial which lay bang in the centre of the road between the front of the City Hall and the Robinson and Cleaver building. Would it go inside the City Hall grounds? If so where? After the exercising of many brain cells and much argy-bargy between Councillors it was decided to place it in its present position on the East side of the grounds. One wonders if the latter day Council expended so much debate and angst when it allowed "Belfast's Big Wheel" to be built nearly on top of the memorial.

Traffic congestion on routes into the city also necessitated changes. Holywood Arches were demolished to allow for road widening and a new approach road – the Sydenham By-Pass was opened. It cost £80,000 and was ahead of its time with a special lane for cyclists.

At least at the opening no-one decided to sing verse one of the hymn specially written for the opening of the then new M1 in England:

"O God of speed whose angel host
Fly with swift pace at Thy command
Control our haste from post to post
And bless the highways of our land."

Perhaps on reflection they should. The spanking new by-pass immediately encountered congestion and traffic jams – an indication that more and more people were able to afford cars.

Money had to be found for slum clearance and building better housing within the city boundary and this issue has been touched on elsewhere in this book. But the impact on inner city communities of housing clearance in areas of Belfast was more than just an issue of new homes.

Nowadays the city has been sort of gentrified into "Quarters" - the Cathedral Quarter, the Titanic Quarter and so on. Old district names do still live on in the inner city areas. We still have The Markets, The Pass, Sandy Row to name just a few. But, in the 1950s there were more areas with their own distinct communities, identities and names – Smithfield, Sailortown, The Marrow Bone, The Hammer, The Pound Loney.

In these inner city areas slum clearance and the provision of better housing was a priority for the Corporation. However, one slum clearance scheme shows how much what seemed to be a move forward in terms of housing affected a particular local community.

The slum clearance scheme in question was that of Upper Library Street. An area made up of Upper Library Street, Peter's Hill, Regent Street, Denmark Street and North Boundary Street. The Council debated the scheme at a meeting held on Friday, 11th September 1959. Many Councillors had strong reservations about the building of flats. Councillor Mrs. Barter [Unionist, Court Ward] prophetically said that if the flats were not properly maintained they would in 10-15 years become like the slums the Council was attempting to replace. Councillors were then told that the flats would be let to childless couples or couples with only one child. Families were to be accommodated in houses. Under the proposed scheme 600 families would be moved from the area. Thus a community where families had lived for generations would be broken up. To St. Patrick's Roman Catholic Church this represented a loss of 2500 members of the congregation!

The desire to keep the community together was not felt to be feasible and the Councillors opted for pragmatism. By 19 votes to 14 the fate of Upper Library Street was sealed. Many other inner city communities would suffer a similar fate of break up or worse. People would be shunted off to housing estates on the margins or stacked in blocks of flats – none more notorious than the Divis Complex. Hindsight is a wonderful thing when judging peoples' actions but in the context of the time the Council believed it was doing its best to modernise the city. Work in the city centre included rebuilding work on bomb-sites in High Street, Bridge Street, Rosemary Street and Ann Street with the biggest challenge the redevelopment of the huge bombsite fronting York Street. On other fronts the Corporation also proved to be energetic.

Strenuous efforts to attract work to the city were made by councillors and successive Lord Mayors who travelled abroad and to the USA to try to drum up jobs for the city.

In 1958 the workers at Shorts' plant at Castlereagh staged an all-night sit-in stating –"We want Work. Work or Starve." That same year the then Chancellor, Heathcott Amery, promised that "local pockets of heavy unemployment must be tackled with all possible energy". Could this help the endangered industries of Belfast? But by the 50s Belfast had to overcome many obstacles in the search for work for its citizens.

In the pamphlet issued to accompany the Ulster Farm and Factory Exhibition at Castlereagh as part of the Festival of Britain, 1951 these optimistic words had appeared:

"In Ulster we are rich in enterprise, limited in basic material. Before we can fire a furnace or lay a keel, **we import the means to do so....**"

The pamphlet went on to extol the fact that in spite of these disadvantages Belfast could in 1951 boast some of the world's top industries. But, read carefully. In these few opening words also lies the biggest problem Belfast's industries faced and why politicians' efforts would ultimately fail to keep the city prosperous. Too many imports and not enough output.

By 1959 Northern Ireland's trade deficit was growing. Per thousand tons Northern Ireland was exporting 334,301 whilst at the same time importing 369,945 and this situation was going to worsen. It is something that playing "partition-politics" would not help. Some Belfast people with get up and go began to do just that.

In December 1958 Australia brought in a £10 air fare scheme for would be emigrants and Belfast people lined up to be "£10 Poms".

Since 1945 22,000 people had emigrated from Northern Ireland. By September 1959 the newly opened Australian Emigration Office in Belfast had had 6000 enquiries, letters and phone calls. Two thousand had been approved for emigration and ninety percent of those opting for a "golden future" were skilled labour or professionals. Hardly any unemployed had applied. A 53 year old ex-R.U.C. Constable, his wife and all of his 11 children emigrated for the princely sum of £20.

Perhaps people were fed up with just making do. They wanted something different and more hopeful. Something more than what had happened in July 1955 when a former IRA internee, Brendan O'Boyle, a member of the militant republican group, Laochra Uladh [Warriors of Ulster] had blown himself up whilst attempting to leave a car bomb at the back gates of Stormont. Surely Australia held out the prospect of something more progressive than Ulster's stodgy, sectarian politics.

The unionists of the 1950s had not softened their attitude to North/South relations and to relations with the minority in Northern Ireland. Brookeborough rebuffed any overtures of goodwill from Southern governments branding any suggestions of concessions to further better relations as, "Lundyism".

The aim of Brookeborough unionism was the maintenance of a rigid Britishness.

For unionists the elections of 1955 and 1959 had presented a worrying change. This was the rise in the number of people voting Sinn Fein. Two members of Sinn Fein had been elected for Westminster seats in 1955 and had to have their wins overturned by legal challenges from the unionists. It was unpredictable with an IRA campaign in full swing in 1959 what way nationalists would direct their votes. However, in the 1959 Westminster election the SF vote fell from the 24% of 1955 to 11%.

Why? Was this a signal of change in nationalist thinking? If it was then it needed to be capitalised on.

As the 50s drew to a close younger unionists like Terence O'Neil began to see that the party's attitudes to others on the island had to be modernised. There had been significant indicators that times were changing as Northern Ireland and Belfast approached the next decade.

In 1958 a conference had been held at Garron Tower at which a leading member of the Roman Catholic laity G.B. Newe had argued that Roman Catholics should instead of detaching themselves from the northern state try to participate in it. In 1959 Sean Lemass replaced de Valera as Taioseach and in a speech in the Oxford Union in October of that year addressed Northern Ireland's constitutional position- the first time a Taioseach had virtually acknowledged the existence of it as a separate state. Would the 1960s be an era of rapprochement in relations between North and South and between the groups within Northern Ireland? Brookeborough's likely acceptance of a changed state of affairs is indicated when in 1959 a suggestion was made that Roman Catholics should be allowed to stand as prospective unionist candidates. He sided with Orange Order opposition to the suggestion and stamped on it at once.

Were the 1950s a successful era in the history of Northern Ireland and Belfast? True there was no upheaval as in the decades to follow. But on what basis was it quiet? People who do not see or acknowledge the inherent weaknesses and problems of the decade will say, "Oh but everybody got on. There was no trouble." Try telling that to those who were subject to the abortive IRA campaign along the border or, to the nationalist minority who felt it had no way of democratically opposing a system it saw as imposed on it.

"One tragic result is that our people have lost faith in democratic institutions. When everybody is busy calling the IRA names, remember that we have many times predicted that the frustration and cynicism of our political life would inevitably lead to violence.............."

Eddie McAteer's words went unheeded with calamitous result in the decades to follow. Isn't hindsight a wonderful thing!

BIBLIOGRAPHY

Bardon J. "Belfast a Century."

Beckett. J.C. and Glasscock. E {Editors] "Origin and Growth of an Industrial City."

Buckland P. "A History of Northern Ireland."

Byrne. O. [Ed] "State of Play: The Theatre and Cultural Identity in Twentieth Century Ulster."

Cathcart R. "A Most Contrary Region. The BBC in Northern Ireland 1924-1984."

Clifford A. "The Mater Hospital [Belfast] and the National Health Service. Past, Present and Future."

Fanning T. "The Fethard-on Sea Boycott."

H.M.S.O. "The Ulster Year Book" 1950-1959.

Hanna Bell S. "The Theatre in Ulster."

Harbinson J. "The Ulster Unionist Party 1882 – 1973."

Harkness D. "Northern Ireland Since 1920."

Harrison R.L. "Population Change and Housing Provision in Belfast."

Hill J. "Cinema and Northern Ireland."

Johnston N. "Austerity Ulster 1947 – 1951."

Jones E. "A Social Geography of Belfast."

Loughlin J. "The Ulster Question Since 1945." [Studies in Contemporary History: Ed. T.G. Fraser and J.D. Springfield]

Maguire W.A. " Belfast."

Marr A. "A History of Modern Britain."

McNeilly N. "Exactly Fifty Years."

Official Handbook "The Festival of Britain in Northern Ireland, 1951."

Open M. "Fading Lights."

U.A.H.S. "Central Belfast: A Historical Gazetter."

Wichert S. "Northern Ireland Since 1945."

Newspaper Sources. 1950-1959

Belfast Newsletter

Belfast Telegraph

Irish News

Northern Whig

The Irish Times